Uncle Vanya

by Anton Chekhov

Adapted by David Mamet

from a translation by
Vlada Chernomordik

A Samuel French Acting Edition

SAMUEL FRENCH

FOUNDED 1830

SAMUELFRENCH.COM

MUSIC USE NOTE

TALKBACK RESTRICTION

IMPORTANT BILLING AND CREDIT REQUIREMENTS

American Repertory Theatre, Cambridge, Mass.
presents

Uncle Vanya

by **ANTON CHEKHOV**
Adapted by **DAVID MAMET**
From a literal translation by
VLADA CHERNOMORDIK

Directed by **DAVID WHEELER**
Sets by **BILL CLARKE**
Costumes by **CATHERINE ZUBER**
Lighting by **THOM PALM**
Sound by **STEPHEN SANTOMENNA**

Major funding for the New Stages Series is provided by Lechmere, Inc.

This production is made possible by generous funding from the
Massachusetts Council on the Arts and Humanities/New Works
Program, the Andrew W. Mellon Foundation, and the DeWitt Wallace-Reader's
Digest Fund, Inc.

The American Repertory Theatre and the Institute for Advanced Theatre Training at Harvard are
supported in part by major grants from the National Endowment for the Arts; the Massachusetts
Council on the Arts and Humanities, a state agency whose funds are recommended by the
Governor and appropriated by the State Legislature, the National Arts Stabilization Fund and the
Greater Boston Arts Fund; the Educational Foundation of America; the Eleanor Naylor Dana Trust; the
Ford Foundation; and the DeWitt Wallace-Reader's Digest Fund. The A.R.T. also gratefully
acknowledges the support of Harvard University, including President Derek C. Bok, Dean A. Michael
Spence, the Committee on Dramatics, the Loeb Visiting Committee, Dean Michael Shinagel, and
the School of Continuing Education, among others. We also wish to give special thanks to our
audience and to the many Friends of the A.R.T. for helping us make this season possible.

UNCLE VANYA

CAST
(in order of speaking)

MARINA, *an old nurse*	**Bronia Stefan Wheeler**
MIKHAIL LVOVICH ASTROV, *a doctor*	**Christopher Walken**
IVAN PETROVICH VOYNITZKY (Vanya), *son of Mariya Vasilyevna Voynitzkaya*	**Daniel Von Bargen**
ALEXANDR VLADIMIROVICH SEREBRYAKOV, *a retired professor*	**Alvin Epstein**
ILYA ILYICH TELEGIN (Waffles), *an impoverished landowner*	**Tim McDonough**
SOFYA ALEXANDROVNA (Sonya), *Serebryakov's daughter*	**Pamela Gien**
YELENA ANDREYEVNA, *Serebryakov's wife, aged 27*	**Lindsay Crouse**
MARIYA VASILYEVNA VOYNITZKAYA, *widow of a privy councilor, mother of Professor's first wife*	**Priscilla Smith**
WORKMAN	**Marty Lodge**

STAGE MANAGERS	**Anne S. King, Abbie H. Katz, Spike Perry**
PRODUCTION ASSOCIATE	**Cynthia Peterson**

Guitar arranged and performed by Paul Sedgwick

ACT I	Early Afternoon, Late June
ACT II	Night, Early July
ACT III	Afternoon, Early September
ACT IV	Evening of the Same Day

The action takes place at Serebryakov's country estate.

There will be one intermission.

CHARACTERS

SEREBRYAKOV, ALEXANDR VLADIMIROVICH, a retired professor

YELENA ANDREYEVNA, his wife, aged twenty-seven

SOFYA ALEXANDROVNA (Sonya), his daughter by first marriage

VOYNITZKAYA, MARIYA VASILYEVNA, widow of a privy councilor, mother of the Professor's first wife

VOYNITZKY, IVAN PETROVICH, her son

ASTROV, MIKHAIL LVOVICH, a doctor

TELEGIN, ILYA ILYICH, an impoverished landowner

MARINA, an old nurse

A WORKMAN

The action takes place on Serebryakov's country estate.

UNCLE VANYA

ACT I

SCENE: A garden. Part of the house and veranda can be seen. Under an old poplar tree in the avenue, a table is set for tea. Benches, chairs; a guitar on one of the benches. Not far from the table, a swing. It is a little past two in the afternoon. Cloudy.

AT RISE: MARINA, a doughy little old lady of little movement, is sitting by the samovar knitting a stocking. ASTROV is walking about close by.

MARINA. *(Pours a glass of tea.)* Drink, Little One.

ASTROV. No. No thank you, I don't want it somehow.

MARINA. A little vodka...?

ASTROV. Not today. No I can't drink it every day. It's not good for me. *Nanny:* How long have we known each other?

MARINA. How long. Lord, let me see: you came here, when? Sonitchka's mother was still with us, then, and you were here the last two winters she was still alive. That's what? Eleven years. More.

ASTROV. How much have I changed?

MARINA. How much?

ASTROV. Yes.

MARINA. Very much. I think. Then you were young, and now you are old. I think your looks are faded...and you're drinking now...

ASTROV. I have become a "different man."

MARINA. That's true.

ASTROV. Why? *(pause)* Why? Overwork, simply. On my feet all day, every day. Every night I go to sleep in fear I'll be called out on a call. In the years you've known me I have not had one single free day. Do you know that? Then how can I help but to become old? You tell me: living such a life. In the midst of people, as you can see, and think of them as "characters..." Time passes, and you notice, bit by bit, you've become one of them. I ask you: look at this moustache. *Why?* To what purpose? I've become some jolly "type." Not *dead* yet, some enthusiasms, some "thoughts," but quite subdued. *(pause)* Dull, somehow. Nothing that I want, no one that I love...Nothing I need...well, I love *you,* of course...When I was young, do you know, I had a nurse who was exactly like you.

MARINA. Eat.

ASTROV. No. Third week of Lent. I was called to Malitzkoye. Spotted fever. There were rows of huts, and people in the huts, side by side on the floor, lying in filth. Cattle living in the buildings with the sick. Young pigs in there, in the same room. All day, working with not a bite to eat. I come home, thank *God,* to lie down. To rest. And they bring in a switchman, hit by the train, and, and I get him on the table, I'm going to start operating, and he dies under the chloroform. Alright, at the moment when I least required it, my conscience chose to inform me that I murdered him. I sat down and I closed my eyes, and thought: One hundred years from now. One hundred years from now: those who come after us. For whom our lives are showing the way. Will they think kindly of us? Will they remember us with a kind word; and, nurse, I wish to God that I could think so.

MARINA. The people won't remember. But God will.

ASTROV. Thank you. *(pause)* That was nicely said.

(Enter IVAN PETROVICH.)

IVAN PETROVICH. ...yes...yes...

ASTROV. Sleep well?

IVAN PETROVICH. Yes. Very. *(yawns)* I'll tell you; since the Herr und Frau Professor've come to visit my life's gone completely off the track. I'm sleeping days, I'm up nights, I'm served all sorts of *je ne sais quoi* to eat, and I don't think it's healthy...I'm drinking *wines*...Used to be, all day, each-moment-ordered: *work...this,* well, well, *Sonya's* still working, of course, but what am *I* doing? Eat. Sleep. Drink. It isn't good.

MARINA. Modern ways.

IVAN PETROVICH. That's absolutely right.

MARINA. Professor sleeps til noon. I keep the samovar boiling all morning. Waiting for him to get up. Before them we ate dinner at noon, eh? Little people everywhere. And now it's after six. He writes and reads all night. Two o'clock in the morning, there's a ring...and what is it? Excuse me: he wants tea. "Wake the house, please, put on the samovar." Modern ways?

ASTROV. And how much longer are they here?

IVAN PETROVICH. A hundred years. He wants to move here.

ASTROV. No...

MARINA. Now; see; here's two hours that the samovar's been on the boil. Where are they...? Outside walking.

IVAN PETROVICH. Well, here they come. Don't fret.

(Voices are heard. SEREBRYAKOV, YELENA ANDREYEVNA, SOFYA, and TELEGIN Enter.)

SEREBRYAKOV. Magnificent. Beautiful views. What a prospect.

TELEGIN. Beautiful, your excellency.

SOFYA. And tomorrow, I'll take you to the plantation, Papa. Would you like that?

IVAN PETROVICH. Ladies and gentlemen: the tea is served.

SEREBRYAKOV. Do you mind? Friends. Would you please send it to my study? I've a few things that I have to do.

SOFYA. ...I know you'll like the plantation. *(Exit YELENA ANDREYEVNA, SEREBRYAKOV and SOFYA.)*

IVAN PETROVICH. It's hot, it's sweltering, and our great scholar dresses for December.

ASTROV. ...Quite a careful man.

IVAN PETROVICH. But she? Magnificent, eh? Now that is a stunning woman. I don't think I've ever seen a more beautiful woman.

TELEGIN. I am so happy. Whatever I do, walk in the garden, look at this table, whatever I do, Marina

Timofeyvna, I do it, and I feel happiness.

MARINA. ...God bless you...

TELEGIN. ...The weather is enchanting, the birds sing, we live in peace and harmony...what else could a man want? *(She passes him a glass of tea.)* Thank you...

IVAN PETROVICH. ...and her *eyes...*

ASTROV. Ivan Petrovich.

IVAN PETROVICH. Yes...

ASTROV. *Tell* us something.

IVAN PETROVICH. What should I tell you?

ASTROV. Tell us something, something *new...*

IVAN PETROVICH. Something new, what's new? Everything is old. Nothing's changed...*I'm* the same...*no,* probably worse, for I have grown *lazy,* and *complain* all day. What's changed...? My Old Crow, my old Mother's still prating on of her dear "Rights of Women," one eye on the grave, the other in her books for the Secret of Life...

ASTROV. ...and our Professor...?

IVAN PETROVICH. The Professor goes on as before. He sits at his desk all day and half of the night and he writes.

"We strain our heart to write our odes,

The mark of it's found on our brow,

But here what praise for them or their progenitor?

No word."

I pity the paper. *(pause)* What is he *doing* there all day? What is he *working* on? Why doesn't he turn to some *magnificent* subject, like, his autobiography, God forbid. Now, *there's* a book: a worked-out academic, a salt cod. A learned *stick...*Gout, rheumatism, migraine, his liver inflamed from jealousy and envy, lives on the estate of his first wife. From choice? Oh, no, because he's too damned cheap to live in town. And this man, constantly prates of his misfortunes. What *are* they? He *has* none. This man lives under a charm. The son of a poor deacon, eh? A scholarship student at the Seminary, gets a degree, he gets a teaching chair, and now he is "Your Excellancy." Marries the daughter of a *Senator,* and *so* on...And I say *forget* that, because *best* of all, this man is so *exceeding* fortunate to write and lecture for twenty-five years upon a subject of which he knows *less* than not-one-thing. Twenty-five years this wise man tells us about Art. Twenty-five years, he reads the works of other and prattles about *realism,* naturalism, specious nonsense which the clever have long known, and which the stupid *do not care about.* He has been going to a dry well with a broken bucket. And yet what self-importance. What pretension. Living in retirement. Not a living soul knows who he is, or cares; nor is he missed from a position which he held twenty-five years. Eh? For a quarter of a century, this man kept some more worthy man out of a job. Yet *look* at him: he walks on Earth like, "Yes, I'm here among you..."

ASTROV. You know, I believe you're jealous.

IVAN PETROVICH. Oh yes. I am jealous. *And* what a success with women...What a Don Juan is this man. Who is his first wife? My sister, a transcendent beauty, pure as the blue sky. Generous, noble, who had more admirers than this man had students, and who, *God* knows why, loved him as only the pure angels love. My mother, his mother-in-law, dotes on him to this day, and *to* this day, he inspires in her reverent awe. His *second* wife, this beauty whom we just saw, a perceptive woman, married him, he was already old, and gave up to him her youth, her beauty, her freedom, her..."luster"...for what? Why? I ask you.

ASTROV. And she stays faithful to him...?

IVAN PETROVICH. Regrettable, yes.

ASTROV. Regrettably?

IVAN PETROVICH. Yes, and I'll tell you why. For a "fidelity" like this is false. From start to close. It is composed of rhetoric, but not of logic, eh? To cheat, to cheat on an old man who revolts you, that is immoral. But to stifle yourself in unhappiness, to willfully squander your youth, we can *commend* that, eh?

TELEGIN. Vanya, please. No, don't speak like that. No, someone who betrayed a wife, or husband, they could just as easily betray, betray...their *country!*

IVAN PETROVICH. Please. You're killing me.

TELEGIN. No, Vanya. Allow me. My wife ran off from me the day after our wedding. *(pause)* I think she didn't like me. Have I, but, did I forget my duty? No. To this day, I love and revere her, and to this day I stay faithful. And I support her all I can. That is, I give her all I have. *(pause)* So that she could raise her children *(pause)* which she got with the man that she loves. Have I given up happiness...? Yes. But I kept my pride. Now, what of her? Her youth is gone. Her beauty, as it must, has faded. Her lover has died. What does she have now?

(Enter SONYA and YELENA ANDREYEVNA, then MARIYA VASILYENA.)

SOFYA. Nanny.

MARINA. Yes.

SOFYA. You go talk to the peasants. I'll see to the tea. *(Exit MARINA.)*

ASTROV. You know, I came to see your husband. You wrote he was deathly ill, with rheumatism, complications, and it seems he's in the perfect pink of health.

YELENA ANDREYEVNA. Last night he was ill.

ASTROV. ...mmm...

YELENA ANDREYEVNA. He complained of his legs. Yes, though, today, you're right, he does seem fine.

ASTROV. He seems fine and I flat-out galloped twenty miles...oh, never mind. It isn't the first time. Alright. I'll stay here tonight, if you don't mind, then, at least, I'll get some sleep.

SOFYA. Oh, lovely, it's so rare that you stay the night here with us. I don't expect you've eaten. Have you?

ASTROV. No. Many thanks, and thank you kindly. No I haven't. No.

SOFYA. Well, then, you'll get your sleep and get your dinner. These days we're not dining until six. *(drinks tea)* Cold tea.

TELEGIN. Yes. The heat in the samovar has markedly decreased.

SOFYA. No matter, Ivan Petrovich, we'll drink it cold.

TELEGIN. Begging your pardon, madam, not Ivan Ivanych, but Ilya Ilyich, Ma'am.

YELENA ANDREYEVNA. "Ilya Ilyich."

TELEGIN. Or, as some have called me "waffles," in referring to my pockmarked face.

YELENA ANDREYEVNA. Waffles?

TELEGIN. Some years ago I had the honor to stand god-father to our Sonetchka, and your husband, His Ex'lency, knows me very well. I'm living here, in the estate now, and you may have noticed, Ma'am, that I have dinner with you every day.

SOFYA. Ilya Ilyich is our Good Right Hand. Some more tea, darling...?

MARIYA VASILYEVNA. ...Ah...

SOFYA. ...Yes...?

MARIYA VASILYEVNA. I forgot to tell Alexander. I received a letter from Kharkohov today. Pavel Alex-eyevitch sent me his new pamphlet.

ASTROV. Yes, and is it interesting?

MARIYA VASILYEVNA. Interesting, yes, but *strange.* He's now refuting the very things he defended seven years ago. How...how...

SOFYA. What?

MARIYA VASILYEVNA. How awful.

IVAN PETROVICH. Nothing awful in it. Happens all the time. Drink your tea, Ma'am.

MARIYA VASILYEVNA. No, I want to talk.

IVAN PETROVICH. We all want to talk. We've been talk-ing, we've been talking the last fifty years. Fifty years we've been reading and writing pamphlets, and I say "enough."

MARIYA VASILYEVNA. Why is it you find it unpleasant to hear me speak? Excuse me, Jean, but you have changed so much in the last year I hardly know you now. You used to be a man of character, a man of fine opinions, an enlightened man. Now,

IVAN PETROVICH. Oh, yes. I was so enlightened, it's unfortunate I lit the way for no one. An enlightened man. What *worse* could you say of me? I am forty seven years of age. Up to one year ago I felt the same as you. I *joyed* to cloud my mind with this, this rank scholasticism...which we *all* hold so dear, and *not* to see real life. I knew that I was doing right. What a fine man! Now...excuse me, if you only knew...

MARIYA VASILYEVNA. ...How can we know if you don't tell us?

IVAN PETROVICH. ...my nights are spent in a vicious fury at the life which I've let slip away from me. I could have enjoyed everything in life. *Everything.* I enjoyed nothing. And now I'm too old.

SOFYA. ...Oh, Uncle...it's depressing...

MARIYA VASILYEVNA. You're blaming, are you blaming your former convictions? What you say is not the fault of your *convictions,* but it's *your* fault. It's your *own* fault. Your convictions by themselves are nothing. Like, like, paint in the palette. It's *you* should have been working, *you,* who should have been *using* them. Doing real work.

IVAN PETROVICH. ...Real work...

MARIYA VASILYEVNA. Yes.

IVAN PETROVICH. Not everyone is called, you know, like your Herr Professor, to go speaking, writing, spewing work forth like some *farm* machine...

MARIYA VASILYEVNA. What do you mean by that?

SOFYA. Grandmother...Uncle Vanya...please...

IVAN PETROVICH. I'm sorry. I'm done. I'm silent. Excuse me. *(pause)*

TELEGIN. What a *lovely* day today. Not too *hot*...

IVAN PETROVICH. Excellent weather for suicide.

MARINA. *(calling the chickens)* Chick chick chick....

——SOFYA. Nanny, why have the peasants come...?

MARINA. Same old thing, the wasteland, again...chick chick chick.

——SOFYA. Which one are you calling?

MARINA. Polkadot. Gone off with her chicks. Don't want to let the crows get them. *(Exits.)*

(TELEGRIN plays the guitar. A WORKMAN Enters.)

WORKMAN. Please, is the doctor here...? *(to ASTROV:)* Please, Mikhail Lvovitch, they're looking for you.

ASTROV. Who?

WORKMAN. From the factory.

ASTROV. Oh, fine. That's fine...well, I have to go. *Dammit... (pause)* What a shame...

——SOFYA. Oh, I'm so sorry. Please come back for dinner.

ASTROV. ...Mmm...

——SOFYA. ...after the factory.

ASTROV. Well, it will be too late, won't it? How could I...how could I...look here, friend, get me a glass of vodka, will you...? *(WORKMAN Exits.)* How...how... *(He finds his cap.)* What's the Ostrovsky play about the man who has a big moustache and small abilities...? That's me. Well. Ladies and gentlemen, I have the honor... *(to YELENA ANDREYEVNA:)* If you should like to stop by some time, perhaps, with Sofia Alexandrovna here, I would be most delighted. There's not a lot to see. I only have the 30 acres; but if it interested you, *next* to me we have a model orchard such as you won't see within 800 miles. The State Plantation; the overseer, the Old Forester, he's usually ill, you see, and actually I get to oversee the work myself.

YELENA ANDREYEVNA. Yes. They told me you loved the woods.

ASTROV. Yes.

YELENA ANDREYEVNA. I suppose there's much good to be done there.

ASTROV. Much good.

YELENA ANDREYEVNA. ...But my question is, doesn't that interfere with your real calling?

ASTROV. My real calling. God knows what our real calling is.

YELENA ANDREYEVNA. The woods. You find it interesting.

ASTROV. Fascinating. Yes.

IVAN PETROVICH. ...Yes, fascinating.

YELENA ANDREYEVNA. *(to ASTROV:)* You don't seem that old. What would we say, thirty six, thirty seven, so... *(pause)* How *interesting* can that be, really, alone in the woods all the time? I should think it quite monotonous.

SOFYA. Oh, not at all, no, it's quite interesting. Every year he plots new forests, or he makes a plan to conserve the old ones. He's received both a medal and a diploma for his work. And if you *listen* to him you'll see what he means. He says that forests *embellish* the land, that they instill in man a love of beauty, that they raise the mind. They moderate the climate; and, in countries with a milder climate, people struggle less with nature. So, in those lands man is milder, gentler. And the people in those lands are more supple and beautiful. Their speech is more refined, their movements are more graceful. *(pause)* They cultivate the arts and sciences...there is joy in their philosophy...they treat women with nobleness...

IVAN PETROVICH. Bravo, bravo...Magnificent. But not convincing. *(to ASTROV:)* My dear, as I must persist in fueling my stoves and building with those same woods that you prize.

ASTROV. Burn peat in your stoves.

IVAN PETROVICH. Mm?

ASTROV. ...Build your barn of stones. You understand? Yes, sometimes we cut wood out of necessity, but why be wanton? Why? Our forests fall before the ax. Billions of trees. All perishing. The homes of birds and beasts being laid waste. The level of the rivers falls, and they dry up. And sublime landscapes disappear, never to return, because man hasn't sense enough to bend down and pick fuel up from the ground. *(to YELENA AN-DREYEVNA:) Isn't* this so? What must man be, to destroy what he never can create? God's given man reason and power of thought, so that he may improve his lot. What have we used these powers for but waste? We have destroyed the forest, our rivers run dry, our wildlife is all but extinct, our climate, ruined, and every day, every day, wherever one looks, our life is more hideous. *(to IVAN PETROVICH:)* I see. You think me amusing. These seem to you the thoughts of some poor eccentric. Perhaps, perhaps it's naive on my part. Perhaps you think that; but I pass by the woods I've saved from the ax. I hear the forest sighing...I *planted* that forest.

And I think; perhaps things *may* be in our power. You understand. Perhaps the climate itself is in our control.

Why not? And if, in one thousand years, man is happy, I will have played a part in that happiness. A small part. I plant a birch tree. I watch it take root, it grows, it sways in the wind, and I feel such pride...

(The WORKMAN Enters with the vodka.)

ASTROV. Well... *(ASTROV takes the vodka. Drinks.)* Well...I must be off. And, of course, it's possible I'm just deluded. Thank you for the honor of your hospitality.

SOFYA. When will you come see us again?

ASTROV. I can't say.

SOFYA. ...But sooner than next month, I hope...? *(They Exit.)*

YELENA ANDREYEVNA. You, Ivan Petrovich, what, have you fallen in one of your "moods" again...?

IVAN PETROVICH. ...Excuse me...?

YELENA ANDREYEVNA. You were being impossible.

IVAN PETROVICH. ...Was I...?

YELENA ANDREYEVNA. Well, yes, you *were*. Why are you baiting your mother...and, today, at breakfast you quarrelled with Alexander.

IVAN PETROVICH. Hmm.

YELENA ANDREYEVNA. Yes. Excuse me. How petty.

IVAN PETROVICH. Petty?

YELENA ANDREYEVNA. Yes.

IVAN PETROVICH. But if I "hate" him...?

YELENA ANDREYEVNA. And why should you hate him? He's like everyone else. He's no worse than you.

IVAN PETROVICH. Oh, please, look at yourself, your face, look at the way you *move*...you are too lazy to *live*, with your "torpor"...

YELENA ANDREYEVNA. "Too lazy to live..."

IVAN PETROVICH. Yes. You are.

YELENA ANDREYEVNA. Yes. I am. And too bored. Do you know? Everyone berates my husband. Everyone berates him. Everybody pities me. "Oh, the poor woman...saddled with such an old man..." They're so *concerned* for me. You must *excuse me, but it's quite disgusting.* Don't *you think so...?* Tell me. What has Astrov said? You cut down woodlands you cannot replace, and soon they will be gone. And *you* cut *men* down. Mindlessly. And soon it will be gone. True feeling...purity, fidelity, self-sacrifice. It will be *gone,* do you understand...? You cannot, you do not, why can you not look with indifference on a woman who is not your own? Why? Because the doctor is right, there is in each one of you a demon of destruction, which spares *nothing:* neither forests, birds, nor women, nor each *other...*

IVAN PETROVICH. Yes. You know, I don't care much for this philosophy. *(pause)*

YELENA ANDREYEVNA. He has a tired face.

IVAN PETROVICH. He?

YELENA ANDREYEVNA. Our doctor.

IVAN PETROVICH. Yes. He does.

YELENA ANDREYEVNA. An interesting face. A nervous face, I think. Sonya finds him attractive. I think she's in love with him. *I* understand it... *(pause)* You know, he's been here three times since I came. And I haven't once spoken with him properly. What do you think? He must think we mean.

IVAN PETROVICH. Must he?

YELENA ANDREYEVNA. Yes. I've never shown him any kindness. Do you know why we are such good friends, Ivan Petrovich?

IVAN PETROVICH. No.

YELENA ANDREYEVNA. ...it's because we are both tiresome people. Yes. We're both dull. Please don't look at me that way. I don't like it.

IVAN PETROVICH. How else can I look at you? I love you. I look and I see my life, my happiness, my youth and I see my life, my happiness, my youth. And I *know* the chances you reciprocate my feelings are nothing. But I want nothing. *(pause)* Only that you permit me to look, to hear your voice...

YELENA ANDREYEVNA. Please. Someone will hear you.

IVAN PETROVICH. Only that you let me speak, to be *near* you...

YELENA ANDREYEVNA. Oh, God, this is awful... *(They Exit.)*

(END OF ACT ONE.)

ACT II

SCENE: The dining room in Serebryakov's house. Night. A watch-man can be heard TAPPING in the garden.

AT RISE: SEREBRYAKOV is sitting in an armchair before the open window, dozing. YELENA ANDREYEVNA is sitting beside him, dozing.

SEREBRYAKOV. *(waking)* Who is it? Sonya? Is that you...?

YELENA ANDREYEVNA. It's me.

SEREBRYAKOV. Lenotchka. I'm in pain. Help me.

YELENA ANDREYEVNA. Your blankets fell. I'll close the window.

SEREBRYAKOV. No. It's *stifling* in here. I dozed off. And I dreamt my leg belonged to someone else. And I was woken by the pain. I don't, I don't think that it's gout. I think it's rheumatism. What time is it?

YELENA ANDREYEVNA. Twenty past twelve.

SEREBRYAKOV. In the morning please go to the library. Look for the "Batuishkov." I think we have him...

YELENA ANDREYEVNA. mmm?

SEREBRYAKOV. Look for... *(pause)* In the morning, please look for Batiushkov. I recall we had him. Why can I not breathe?

YELENA ANDREYEVNA. Two nights with no sleep... you're tired.

23

SEREBRYAKOV. They say Turgenyev developed angina pectoris from gout. Eh? And I'll get it too. *Damn* old age. Damn revolting, impotent old age. Damn it. I am old, and grow repulsive to myself, and I'm sure you, too, find it revolting to look on me.

YELENA ANDREYEVNA. Do you know, you talk of your age in a tone that suggests it's our fault that you've grown old.

SEREBRYAKOV. ...And I revolt you most of all. *(YELENA ANDREYEVNA moves farther away from him.)* And you're right, of course. I'm not stupid. I understand. You are young, you're healthy, and you're beautiful. You want to live and here am I, an old man, more than one foot in the grave. Isn't that right? Of *course* that's right. How *foolish* I must feel, eh, to be still living. But be patient. Soon I will set you all free. I give my word. A little longer...

YELENA ANDREYEVNA. Oh, God, please, I'm ready to collapse. What must I do? *Please* be silent.

SEREBRYAKOV. Yes, Yes, Yes! Thanks to me, you're *all* ready to collapse. All of you. Everyone *bored.* ...Wasting their youth...*I'm* the only one content. I see it...

YELENA ANDREYEVNA. Be still! You're *destroying* me.

SEREBRYAKOV. Oh, yes. I'm destroying *everyone*...of *course*...

YELENA ANDREYEVNA. What do you want from me?

SEREBRYAKOV. Nothing.

YELENA ANDREYEVNA. Well, then, be quiet. Will you please? I beg you.

SEREBRYAKOV. I'll tell you a most peculiar thing. Ivan Petrovich, that *dolt,* or Mariya Vasilyevna, they begin holding forth, it's *fine.* Everyone listens, everyone is rapt attention. I say *one word* and the *world* feels utterly depressed. You understand? The mere fact of my *voice* they find repulsive. Fine. fine. Let us *stipulate: I am* repulsive. I am a despot. I am that sick egoist you all feel me to be. Have I not earned it? Have I not, *am* I not, I ask you, entitled to this, a peaceful old age? And the least modicum of consideration from those around me?

YELENA ANDREYEVNA. No one disputes your right. *(pause)*

SEREBRYAKOV. I have worked my whole life for science. Respected and honored. I have felt the simple pleasures. Ones *study,* do you know, and the *lecture* halls...the warm respect of one's peers...And then I'm thrust. Thrust. For no apparent reason, in this tomb. Among the mindless. Every day, their prattle stuffing my ears. I want to live. I've worked for these things. For success, recognition, *action*...here I am in exile. Every waking moment. I can pine for the past. I can envy the success of others. Or I can fear death. And those three choices are my life. I cannot...I cannot...God. And they begrudge me even my old age.

YELENA ANDREYEVNA. Have patience. Five or six more years, I'll be old, too.

SOFYA. *(Entering)* Papa, you sent for Dr. Astrov, now he's here and you don't want him. Please what do I tell him now we've put him out for nothing?

SEREBRYAKOV. And what good can Astrov do me? The man knows as much of medicine as I do of beekeeping.

SOFYA. What am I to do, please? We sent for him.

SEREBRYAKOV. He's a fool, and I won't speak to him.

SOFYA. As you wish, then. *(sits)* Fine.

SEREBRYAKOV. What time is it, please?

YELENA ANDREYEVNA. Almost one.

SEREBRYAKOV. I can't breathe. Sonya, please. My drops on the table...

SOFYA. Just a moment... *(She gets the drops and hands them to him.)*

SEREBRYAKOV. Not these! The drops that I *asked* for...for God's sake...

SOFYA. Some may appreciate this peevishness. I don't. Please spare me. I don't like it, I haven't the *time,* I need my rest, tomorrow is a working day...

(Enter IVAN PETROVICH.)

IVAN PETROVICH. A storm brewing outside.

(LIGHTNING.)

IVAN PETROVICH. And will you look at that...! Helene and Sonya: off to bed, you are relieved.

SEREBRYAKOV. Don't leave me with him, he'll talk me to death.

IVAN PETROVICH. ...They need their rest.

SEREBRYAKOV. No.

IVAN PETROVICH. They need their rest. Two nights without sleep...

SEREBRYAKOV. Alright. Fine. The two of them to bed. And you, too. With my thanks. Sincerely. But I beg you, for our friendship's sake; please, leave me alone.

IVAN PETROVICH. For...?

SEREBRYAKOV. ...And we'll talk later.

IVAN PETROVICH. For our "friendship?" Our...?

SOFYA. Ssssshhhhhh, Uncle Vanya...

SEREBRYAKOV. (to YELENA ANDREYEVNA:) No, my dear. Don't leave me with him. I'm quite serious, I...

IVAN PETROVICH. Do you know, this is becoming *funny*...

(Enter MARINA with a candle.)

SOFYA. Nanny. You ought to be in bed. It's late.

MARINA. Well, fine. The *samovar* is on the table...easy to say "go to bed"...

SEREBRYAKOV. Everyone's up. Everyone is fatigued beyond measure. I alone am happy. I'm in ecstasy.

MARINA. (to SEREBRYAKOV:) What is it, Little Father...the legs...? My legs hurt me, too. I have the 'ralgia. 'Ralgia all the day. Your old complaint. I know. Vera Petrovna. Rest in peace. Sonetchka's sainted mother, took it so to heart when you hurt. You know that she did, she loved you so, that woman... *(pause)* The old are like the young. They want someone to pity them. But no one's ever sorry for the old. You go to sleep now, little one. I'll get your linden Tea. And I'll warm your feet, yes I will. And I will pray for you.

SEREBRYAKOV. *(pause, softly)* Oh, go on...

MARINA. ...I have the 'ralgia, too. I have it, too; a pain in my legs. Vera Petrovna would cry. Anyone's pain moved her. Sonetchka, then, such a little one. come along, my little father, now we're going to go to bed. That's right... *(SEREBRYAKOV, SOFYA, and MARINA Exit.)*

YELENA ANDREYEVNA. I've been so tired by him I can hardly stand.

IVAN PETROVICH. Well. You're tired by him and I'm sick of myself. This is my third night without sleep. I'm tired to nausea. *(pause)*

YELENA ANDREYEVNA. This is not a happy home. Your mother loathes everything in this world except her dear pamphlets. And the Professor. The Professor mistrusts me. He fears you...

IVAN PETROVICH. ...He fears me...?

YELENA ANDREYEVNA. Yes. He does. Sonya is angry with her father. Pettish with me, hasn't spoken to me in the last two weeks...Not one word. And you hate my husband. You despise your mother and you make no effort to conceal it. I go around, twenty times a day. I'm on the edge of tears...one would not say this is a happy home.

IVAN PETROVICH. Let's drop this discourse, shall we...?

YELENA ANDREYEVNA. Ivan Petrovich *(pause)* are you an educated man. A thoughtful man and I would expect you to see, or to accept, if you *thought* of it...

IVAN PETROVICH. ...I'm listening.

YELENA ANDREYEVNA. That our world is worsened...not by *fires,* or *robbers*...but, you understand? By *hate.* Our world's destroyed by *hate.* By *pettiness.* And *your* job should be to be *strong* and *not* to carp at those around you. *Not* to grumble, but, simply, to *reconcile*...to make peace...to...

IVAN PETROVICH. I'd make my peace with *you*... *(He tries to kiss her hand.)*

YELENA ANDREYEVNA. Stop it right now! *(pause)* I'd like it if you left now, please.

IVAN PETROVICH. And, yes, the rain is ending. Everything will be refreshed. The world exhales. But I shall *not* be refreshed by the coming and the passing of the storm. My whole life, day and night, I feel this. I've squandered my past on nonsense and my present is sunk in absurdity. Isn't that something? My one feeling is for you. Can I renounce it? My one feeling in life and it's dying like a ray of sun shone in a well. And I am dying.

YELENA ANDREYEVNA. You speak to me of love. How am I to deal with that? I don't know. I'm sorry, but it's true. What do you expect? I'm sorry. Forgive me. I must say goodnight.

IVAN PETROVICH. ...Coincidentally, though, here by my side, another life is being wasted in this house. Whose could that be? What are you waiting for...? Eh? For your *life* to end? What stupid, pointless *principle* stands in your way? You *wastrel.* You *fool,* eh? Do you comprehend what I'm *telling* you...? *(pause)*

YELENA ANDREYEVNA. Ivan Petrovich...are you drunk?

IVAN PETROVICH. It very well could be.

YELENA ANDREYEVNA. Where is the doctor?

IVAN PETROVICH. He's spending the night in my room. It could be. It could be, *anything* could be.

YELENA ANDREYEVNA. And why have you been drinking?

IVAN PETROVICH. Why? Because it seems like "life." Don't scold me, Helene.

YELENA ANDREYEVNA. *(pause)* You never used to drink?

IVAN PETROVICH. I drink now.

YELENA ANDREYEVNA. No, and you never "spoke" so much.

IVAN PETROVICH. I *didn't...?* Perhaps th...

YELENA ANDREYEVNA. ...Go to bed. You bore me.

IVAN PETROVICH. *Do? (kissing her hand)* My enchanted one, my darling...

YELENA ANDREYEVNA. Oh, *please,* oh *please. Oh, God, you disgust me... (Exits.)*

IVAN PETROVICH. Aha. *(pause)* Ten years ago, I'd see her at my sister's. She was seventeen and I was thirty-seven. I could have proposed to her and now she'd be my wife. And both of us would have been woken by the storm. The thunder frightened you. Sshhhh. No, no, no. I'm here. *I'm* here, and you needn't be afraid. And she...Why in the name of God am I old...? What's *happened* to me...? And with her damned pseudo-morality, her lazy, stupid "intellect," her jargon notions of "the ruin of the world"...Who the *hell* does she think she is...? They *cheated* me. I *worshipped* that man. That pitiful pox-ridden "academic," our Professor, and worked like a slave for him. Sonya... *(pause)* And we squeezed the last *dregs* from this estate, like slaves. We sold the *vegetable* oil...we sold the *curds,* the peas, we begrudged ourselves *food* to save half-kopecks, and sent *thousands* to him. Why shouldn't we? As proud as we were... *(pause)* To a man of genius. We basked in him. Now the man retires, and it's *screamingly* clear; what does he leave? As his legacy? This colossus? What *work?* What...what...? He leaves *nothing.* Not a single *page.* A *nothing.* Unknown. *(pause)* A fraud. A vicious failure, who cheated a man who loved him.

ASTROV Enters, somewhat drunk. TELEGIN Enters with a guitar.)

ASTROV. Play something.

TELEGIN. But the house is asleep, sir.

ASTROV. Play it. *(to IVAN PETROVICH:)* Oh. All alone...? No ladies, eh? *(sings)*
"The house is flying
The stove is flying
Where can the master make his bed...?"
Storm woke me. Some rain. What's the time, eh?

IVAN PETROVICH. I don't give a damn.

ASTROV. I heard Yelena Andreyevna...?

IVAN PETROVICH. Very probably

ASTROV. A splendid woman. *(He examines medicine bottles on the table.)* "Lord help us when doctors disagree." *Is* there a town whose pharmacy's not represented her...? The whole region must be sick of his gout. You tell me; is he ill, or shamming?

IVAN PETROVICH. He's ill. *(pause)*

ASTROV. And you? What's *your* complaint? A sympathetic nature?

IVAN PETROVICH. We are just friends.

ASTROV. *Already...*

IVAN PETROVICH. Now what *can* that mean?

ASTROV. A woman and a man can be friends only and the end-term of this sequence; first, acquaintances; then lovers, and then, that's right, "friends."

IVAN PETROVICH. A lovely, elegant philosophy.

ASTROV. Think so? Yes. I confess. I'm becoming a vulgarian. I'm drunk, too. I'll tell you; *normally* I drink

this much just once-a-month. And when I *am* this drunk,
I become arrogant and brazen to the last degree. And
nothing in that state can faze me, then. I undertake and
perform the most difficult feats, *flawlessly.* I see the *future*,
and devise the most elegant plans. And *during* this time I
no longer seem to myself an awkward and useless mem-
ber of the world. No, I seem, on the contrary, a powerful,
a motive force, with my own system of thought, and
philosophy, and *all* of you, my dears, for it's true, look as
big as *microbes,* or some quite, quite unimportant things.
(to TELEGIN:) Would you play, please...?

TELEGIN. My friend, as you know, for you, anything,
but they're all asleep...

ASTROV. Play. *(TELEGIN plays quietly.)* Let's have a
drink. Come on, for I *know* there's some left. And then at
daylight we'll go to my place. Up for it? Fellow works for
me says that the whole time. "Up for it?" Not a nice man.
"Y'up for it...?"

(He sees the entering SONYA.)

ASTROV.   Excuse   me,   I'm   undressed.   *(Exits.
TELEGIN follows.)*

SOFYA. Uncle Vanya...

IVAN PETROVICH. ...As you will.

SOFYA. You've got drunk with the doctor again. Two
free voices. Found each other in the wild. And formed a
pact. *Why* do you do this? At your age...? You know, it's
truly unattractive.

IVAN PETROVICH. My age doesn't figure in it.

SOFYA. ...No...?

IVAN PETROVICH. A man with *nothing*. With no real life; subsists on fantasy and then that's something in his life.

SOFYA. The hay's cut. Every day it rains. And everything is rotten and you live on fantasy. You've thrown your work up and I'm working alone. I'm *tired.* You neglect your *job,* you. Uncle, are you crying?

IVAN PETROVICH. I'm not crying.

SOFYA. I see the tears in your eyes.

IVAN PETROVICH. Just now, do you know, you looked at me, just like your dear mother. *(Kisses SONYA'S hands and cheeks.)* Oh, my darling sister. Where are you now, oh, my dear? If you only knew.

SOFYA. ...What is it she should know?

IVAN PETROVICH. ...It's not good. It's not good. It's nothing. *(pause)* I'm going. *(Exits. Pause.)*

SOFYA. Mikhail Lvovich... *(She knocks on his door.)* You're not asleep...?

ASTROV. *(off)* ...Hello.

SOFYA. May I *speak* with you? *(He Enters)* If it aids you to drink, *please* drink. But I beg of you, *please,* do not let my uncle drink. It's *so* bad for him.

ASTROV. So be it. We'll drink no more.

SOFYA. ...I can count on you...?

ASTROV. Settled and signed. And now I'll be getting home. *(yawns)* By the time they've harnessed, the sun will be up.

SOFYA. Why not wait til morning...

ASTROV. ...Oh no... *(yawns)*

SOFYA. It's raining.

ASTROV. Storm'll pass. I think that this is the end of it.

No, I'll go. One thing, please don't call me for your father anymore. I tell him "gout," and he says "rheumatism." I say "stay in bed," and he gets up. I'm called to see him and he won't speak to me.

SOFYA. He's difficult. *(pause)* Can I get you something to eat?

ASTROV. Yes. I'll take something. Thank you.

SOFYA. They say that through his life he had a great success with women, and that women spoiled him. Here, have some cheese. *(They both stand at the sideboard, eating.)*

ASTROV. Today I didn't eat a thing. Today I drank. Yes, your father is difficult. *(of liquor)* May I...? You know, we're alone here. Let me speak candidly, do you think? I couldn't live one month in this house. With your father and his gout, and your uncle and his, what is it? *Depression...? Your grandmother...* your *stepmother...*

SOFYA. ...My stepmother...

ASTROV. It's nice, and it should be godly to have beauty. Beauty should be pure. Of face, of dress, of the mind, and here is a beauitful, a lovely woman, all she does is eat, sleep, and stroll through the day, to enchant us with that great beauty which is hers. She does no more. She has no *duties;* she has no *responsibilities,* others work *for* her. *(pause)* How can an idle life be pure? Am I too hard? Perhaps I am. I'm like your Uncle Vanya. Disappointed in life, become a detractor.

SOFYA. ...Disappointed? In life?

ASTROV. In life? No. In *our* life. Our provincial and our Russian life. I hate it with the power of my soul. And *my* life. Oh, yes, my own personal life. I am pleased to swear to God there is not one thing good in it. When you walk through the woods, if you walk through the dark woods at night, if you have a *glimmer,* a small *gleam* of light before you, then you needn't fell the night, nor darkness, *fatigue,* nor the branches as they whip your face. But I, as you know, work alone, and live alone. There is no one. And those things which assail me...as there *is* no light before me, which could make my burden light. *(pause)* So I expect nothing. And there is nothing for me. And, do you know, I don't *like* people. And, for the longest time, have loved no one. *(pause)*

SOFYA. You have loved no one.

ASTROV. No. I feel a certain *affection*...I feel affection, for example, toward your nurse.

SOFYA. ...You do...

ASTROV. Yes. Our *peasants* are so alive, living in squalor; what do *we* live in? Our "intelligentsia"...? Our good and stupid friends, to put it bluntly, you see? Small concerns, small thoughts and feelings. And the brighter they are then the worse they are. Assailed by introspection. And analysis, what's *happened* to the world...? They whine, and spew, and slander, "oh, *this* one's a psychopath," or "that's one's a *phrasemonger*..." And let them find someone whom they can't pigeonhole, and he's "a most peculiar man." I love the forest and I don't eat meat. "A most peculiar man." *Where* could we look to find a simple, unencumbered and *spontaneous* relation to our fellows, and the world? Where? *No* where. No where on this earth. *(He starts to drink.)* I *assure* you.

SOFYA. Please, no more. Please. Don't drink.

ASTROV. Why not?

—SOFYA. It isn't like you.

ASTROV. Is that what you think?

—SOFYA. You're refined. And you have a gentle voice. You, more than anyone I know, are as you spoke of, beautiful. *(pause)* Why do you act in an ordinary way?

ASTROV. I...?

—SOFYA. You drink, and you *gamble...*

ASTROV. Do I...?

—SOFYA. Please stop. You say that people don't work to create but to *destroy* those gifts they are given from above. Don't do it. You don't have to do it. Please. Please. I implore you. Please. *(pause)*

ASTROV. I won't drink.

—SOFYA. You won't drink again. *(pause)*

ASTROV. No.

—SOFYA. Give me your word of honor.

ASTROV. I give it.

—SOFYA. Thank you.

ASTROV. *Basta!* eh? I've sobered up. Look at that. Sober already. And I shall *stay* so. As I have vowed. Till the end of my days. *(Looks at his watch.)* Well. So. My time has passed. I'm old, I'm jaded. I am overworked. My feelings are blunt. I have lost capacity for all attachment. What attracts me? What attracts me? Beauty attracts me. I can't remain indifferent to it. Yelena Andreyevna, for example, you see, she'd turn my head in a day. But *that's* not love, now, *is* it...? *(He shudders.)*

—SOFYA. What is it?

ASTROV. It's nothing.

—SOFYA. What is it?

ASTROV. You know, in Lent, I had a patient die under

the chloroform.

SOFYA. It's time you forgot it. *(pause)* If... *(pause)* Would you tell me, Mikhail Lvovich, if a *friend* of mine, if I had such a friend or younger *sister* of mine, and you, suppose, you discovered that this girl *loved* you; *(pause)* what would that make you feel...?

ASTROV. *(pause)* I have no idea. I would suspect that I wouldn't feel a thing.

SOFYA. ...You'd feel nothing?

ASTROV. I think, what I think is I'd give her to understand how I could never *love* her. Uhhh...could you perhaps ask me this later? If I *am* to go I *must* go; and now is the time. Farewell, My *dove*; if we keep talking we will be talking at noon. I'll go out through the drawing room if you permit me, or I fear your uncle would detain me here. Goodbye. *(Exits.)*

SOFYA. *(pause)* He's told me nothing. Yet I'm happy. He keeps his heart and his soul from me. And yet I'm happy and I don't care. Why am I so happy? "A beautiful man," I said; "You have a lovely voice." Was that forward of me? And I don't care. I don't think so, I love his voice. Why shouldn't I? And yet. I spoke to him about my friend. "A younger sister," and he didn't understand a word. Oh, Lord. How could you make me so plain...? Last Sunday at church the woman behind me said, "She's so kind and generous. It's such a pity she's so plain..." *(pause)* ...That she is so plain...

(Enter YELENA ANDREYEVNA.)

SOFYA. End of the storm. Such a peace in the air.

YELENA ANDREYEVNA. *(pause)* Where's the doctor?

SOFYA. Gone.

YELENA ANDREYEVNA. Sophie...

SOFYA. What?

YELENA ANDREYEVNA. How long are you going to go on being short with me? *(pause)* We've done no harm to each other. Why should we be enemies? *(pause)* Don't you feel...? *(pause)* Enough.

SOFYA. I...

YELENA ANDREYEVNA. ...Yes...?

SOFYA. ...I wanted to ...

YELENA ANDREYEVNA. ...I did, too...

SOFYA. Let's not be angry anymore.

YELENA ANDREYEVNA. With all my heart. *(They embrace. sighs.)* Oh, Lord. That's good. *Thank* you.

SOFYA. Has Papa gone to bed?

YELENA ANDREYEVNA. No, he's still sitting up. Weeks at a time we don't speak to each other. God only knows why. *(of the sideboard:)* What's this?

SOFYA. Mikhail Lvovich was having some supper.

YELENA ANDREYEVNA. Drink with me.

SOFYA. Yes.

YELENA ANDREYEVNA. Brundershaft — out of the same glass — Will you kiss me...? *(YELENA ANDREYEVNA fills the glass.)*

SOFYA. I will. *(They drink and kiss.)* I've wanted to make it up for so long. I've felt ashamed. *(SOFYA ALEXAN-DROVNA cries.)*

YELENA ANDREYEVNA. Why are you crying...? Shhhh...

SOFYA. It's alright. It's nothing.

YELENA ANDREYEVNA. Shhh. Shhh. There now...Lord;

I'm crying too. *(pause)* You were...*angry* with me because you think I married your father for my own convenience. If you believe oaths I give you my oath on this; that I married him for love. I was drawn to him. A famous man. A man of learning. I was *captivated* by it. And it was not real. *(pause)* The love was not real. But I *thought* it was real. At the time I *thought* it was real. And I'm not to blame. Sophie. But. *(pause)* Since our wedding day you haven't stopped accusing me.

SOFYA. ...I accused you...?

YELENA ANDREYEVNA. You did. *(pause)* I saw it in your eyes. Your clever and suspicious eyes...looking on...

SOFYA. ...And now we forget it.

YELENA ANDREYEVNA. ...you mustn't look like that on people. It doesn't suit you. And we must *trust.* How can we live if we do not?

SOFYA. I have to ask you. *Honestly...*

YELENA ANDREYEVNA. ...Yes?

SOFYA. ...As a friend.

YELENA ANDREYEVNA. Yes.

SOFYA. Are you happy?

YELENA ANDREYEVNA. No.

SOFYA. I knew that. And now, honestly, would you have preferred to have had a younger husband?

YELENA ANDREYEVNA. What a schoolgirl you are.

SOFYA. Would you?

YELENA ANDREYEVNA. Yes, I should have liked that. Alright, then, what else?

SOFYA. Do you like the doctor?

YELENA ANDREYEVNA. Very much.

SOFYA. *(laughs)* Do I look foolish? Do I? I'm sure that I

do. Do you know, though he's gone, I hear his voice, I
do. I hear his footsteps, and if I look over by the dark window I see him there. Let me say it. I shouldn't say it so
loud. Oh, I feel ashamed. Should we talk in my room?
Do I seem silly to you? Yes, of *course* I do. *Tell* me
about him.

YELENA ANDREYEVNA. What should I tell?

SOFYA. *Isn't* he so clever? *Isn't* he? *Beyond* that; he can *do*
things. He *heals;* he *heals* people...he *plants...* *(pause)*

YELENA ANDREYEVNA. My dear. It's so much more
than that.

SOFYA. It is?

YELENA ANDREYEVNA. It isn't trees...it isn't "forests"
..."medicine..."

SOFYA. ...No...

YELENA ANDREYEVNA. What he has is *talent.* Darling.
Scope-of-Mind. He plants a tree, and when he plants it he
sees, he is trying to see what comes of his action in a thousand years. A thousand years. D'you know? He's thinking of the Happiness of Man. When you *find* such
beautiful people...

SOFYA. ...Yes...?

YELENA ANDREYEVNA. They must be loved. He
drinks...

SOFYA. Yes. He does.

YELENA ANDREYEVNA. ...And he can be *coarse. Coarse.* A
man of soul in Russian cannot remain spotless. *Show* this
man to me. I say "what *of* it...?" if you think of his life. On
the impassable roads. And freezing day and night...vast
distances...He ministers to crude, barbarous folk. Their
poverty, their ignorance around him constantly. Dis-

ease... *(pause)* A man who lives that life... *(pause)* I wish you this happiness, with all my soul. You deserve it. You deserve happiness. *(rises)* I am a dull second-rank character. You know? In *music.* In my husband's *house.* In my love affairs. Throughout my whole life. That is what I've been. *Yes,* as a matter of fact, when you come to think of it, I am quite *thoroughly* unhappy. And I will never find it in this world. Why are you laughing?

SOFYA. I feel so good. *(pause)*

YELENA ANDREYEVNA. Would you like me to play something?

SOFYA. Very much.

YELENA ANDREYEVNA. Yes?

SOFYA. I can't sleep. Play.

YELENA ANDREYEVNA. Good. Go ask your father. When he's ill, music sometimes upsets him. If it's alright then I'll play.

SOFYA. Good. *(Exits.)*

YELENA ANDREYEVNA. So long since I played. I'll play and then I'll cry. *(pause)* Like some damned fool. *(O.S. The sound of the watchman making his rounds.)* Is that you outside, Yefir?

YEFIR. *(O.S.)* It's me.

YELENA ANDREYEVNA. Stop it, please. The master is not well.

YEFIR. I'll stop at once. *(Calls to his dogs.)* Hey there, come on, Dog... *(whistles)*

SOFYA. *(Sofya reenters.)* He says that we can't.

(END OF ACT II)

ACT III

SCENE: The drawing room in Serebryakov's house. Daytime.

AT RISE: IVAN PETROVICH and SOFYA ALEXAN-
DROVNA are seated. YELENA ANDREYEVNA paces
the room.

IVAN PETROVICH. The Herr Professor has been so good
as to express this; that he wishes that we should gather in
this drawing room, at one o'clock this afternoon, *(He*
checks his watch.) that being in one quarter-hour. At which
time he has some *"thing"* which he wishes to share with
the world.

YELENA ANDREYEVNA. Some business matter, probably.

IVAN PETROVICH. But what business? He has none anymore. He writes garbage, he grumbles, he envies the
world, and that's his life.

——SOFYA. ...*Uncle!*

IVAN PETROVICH. Alright. alright. You're right. *Ecco**
how, she walks this woman. Eh? Morbid with laziness. A
panorama of inaction. *Bella.*

YELENA ANDREYEVNA. Must you *prate* all day. Must you
go on always? I'm *dying* of boredom. *Is* there nothing
to do?

Editor's Note: Italian: Look! See!

42

SOFYA. There's no lack of things to do. If you wished to *do* them.

YELENA ANDREYEVNA. *Tell* me one.

SOFYA. Teach. Treat the sick. Care for the estate.

YELENA ANDREYEVNA. ...mmm...mmm...

SOFYA. Much to do. *(pause)* When you and Papa weren't here, Uncle and I would go to the market and sell flour.

YELENA ANDREYEVNA. I wouldn't know how. And, besides, it doesn't interest me. In ideolgical novels people jump up and declare they're going to "teach," or "treat the sick." But how should I do that? Just, suddenly...just...

SOFYA. If you *did* it, you'd be *drawn* to it. Oh, yes, my darling. *(They embrace. SOFYA ALEXANDROVNA laughs.)* You're bored. You don't know what to do. there's no end to it. I know. It's so contagious. Uncle *Vanya* has it, now. And *he* does nothing. And follows you like a cloud on a leash. I put my *own* work down and come over to chat. I've grown so lazy. And our *doctor,* Mikhail Lvovich, who came once a month, if *that,* is here every day. And turns his back both on his forests, and his *medicine.* And lives under your spell.

YELENA ANDREYEVNA. ...My spell?

SOFYA. You *sorcerer!*

IVAN PETROVICH. Oh, but why are you languishing? My dear? My splendor? Awaken and pulse with life. You, when the blood of *mermaids* courses in your veins...wake to your mermaid life! Rise to the heights and plunge into the frothy brine. Love with a water-spirit waits you. In your guise as Naiad of Perfection. So our Herr Professor, so that *all* of us throw up our heads and say, "Who is that nymph?"

YELENA ANDREYEVNA. Oh, will you shut up?

IVAN PETROVICH. ...Did I...?

YELENA ANDREYEVNA. This cruel...cruel...

IVAN PETROVICH. Forgive me. My joy. Forgive me. I apologize. Forgive me. Peace.

YELENA ANDREYEVNA. An Angel of Patience would become short with you.

IVAN PETROVICH. ...As a peace offering...

YELENA ANDREYEVNA. ...*Admit* it.

IVAN PETROVICH. ...As as offering of peace. I'm going to present you with a bouquet of roses, which flowers I have had the foresight to've obtained this morning. Autumn roses. Sad roses. For you. *(Exits.)*

SOFYA. ...Sad autumn roses...

YELENA ANDREYEVNA. Already September. How are we to live through one more winter here? Where is the doctor?

SOFYA. Uncle Vanya's room. He's writing something. I'm glad Uncle's gone. I have to talk with you.

YELENA ANDREYEVNA. About what?

SOFYA. About what. *(pause)* About what...?

YELENA ANDREYEVNA. ...There...there...

SOFYA. I'm plain.

YELENA ANDREYEVNA. You have beautiful hair.

SOFYA. No! No! The homely woman's told "Oh, what beautiful hair." I've loved him for six years. I love him more than I love my own mother. I hear him every moment and I feel his hand. I look at the door and I think, "At any moment..." I keep coming to you about

him, he's here, he looks right through me; I have no hope
and I *know* it. Oh, God, give me strength. All night I pray.
I can't *stop* myself from going up to him. I look in his eyes.
I confessed yesterday to Uncle Vanya. All the servants
know I love him. Everybody knows. *(pause)*

YELENA ANDREYEVNA. What does "he" think?

SOFYA. He doesn't notice me.

YELENA ANDREYEVNA. Aha. You know, he's a strange
man. Do you know what? If...let me approach him. I'll be
discrete. A most gentle hint. What do you think? Really,
how long are you to live in uncertainty? *(pause)* Yes?
(SOFYA ALEXANDROVNA nods.) Good. The question; he
loves you, or doesn't, and can that be hard to know?
Now, don't you be embarrassed, my girl. Don't you
worry. I'll be very gentle, and I'll find the answer. I'll
probe him, and he will never know. Yes. Or no. and if it's
"no," then let him stop coming here. Yes? *(Pause. SOFYA
ALEXANDROVNA nods.)* I *think* so. Yes. Alright. Well,
then, "Well begun is nearly done." We'll put the question. He was going to show me some maps. Tell him that
I want him.

SOFYA. You'll tell me the truth?

YELENA ANDREYEVNA. I will, because I think the *truth,* no
matter how bad, is never so bad as an uncertainty. I pro-
mise you.

SOFYA. You wish to see his maps.

YELENA ANDREYEVNA. That's right.

SOFYA. But in uncertainty, at least...

YELENA ANDREYEVNA. ...Yes?

SOFYA. ...Is hope.

YELENA ANDREYEVNA. Excuse me...?

SOFYA. No. *(pause)* You're right. *(Exits.)*

YELENA ANDREYEVNA. *Lord.* Lord. what is worse than knowing someone's secret and standing by powerless? Clearly the man cares nothing for her. But why shouldn't he take her? Granted. She isn't beautiful. But for a country doctor, his age, a kind, pure, intelligent girl — what's wrong with her for a wife? N'thing. Not a thing. Poor child. *(pause)* Live in a grey world like this, and you hear nothing but the *banal* all day. What everyone eats, drinks, *thinks*...And then this *man* appears. A captivating man, a handsome man...like a bright-colored moon rose from the trees. To *yield* to such a man... *(pause)* Vanya said "Mermaid's blood runs in your veins. For once in your life indulge yourself." Well. *Should* I not do that? For once in my life...? As the man said, once in my life, and fly away from all these sleepy countenances, these dull faces, this sameness, this death-in-life, why shouldn't I? Great coward that I am, when the man comes here *everyday* and I know everyday the reason that he comes? Oh, God, I'm stained already, and I should fall on my knees to Sonya and beg for forgiveness.

(ASTROV Enters.)

ASTROV. Good morning.

YELENA ANDREYEVNA. Good morning.

ASTROV. You wanted to see my drawings.

YELENA ANDREYEVNA. Yesterday you said you'd show me some maps you were working on.

ASTROV. I have them.

YELENA ANDREYEVNA. Are you free?

ASTROV. I am. Where were you born?

YELENA ANDREYEVNA. In Petersburg.

ASTROV. Mm. And where did you study?

YELENA ANDREYEVNA. The Conservatory.

ASTROV. You may find that this won't interest you.

YELENA ANDREYEVNA. Well, no? Why not...? It's true that I don't know the *country...*

ASTROV. ...mmm...hhhm...

YELENA ANDREYEVNA. ...The "topography..."

ASTROV. ...Indeed...

YELENA ANDREYEVNA. But I've *read* a great deal, I...

ASTROV. I have my own work table in this house. In Ivan Petrovich's room, and when I am on the point of extreme exhaustion, I forsake my practice and I steal away to spend an hour or two over my maps. Ivan Petrovich and Sofya Alexandrovna clicking away at the abacus, and I'm seated beside them at my worktable painting. *(pause)* And, I'm warm. Everything is quiet. I'm at peace. I hear the *crickets* outside. Totally at peace. Once a month, perhaps, not so very often. *(Pause. Of his maps.)* Alright. Look here; we have our district fifty years ago. The dark and light greens indicate the forests. As you see, half of the whole is wooded. Now; where we find green crosshatched with red we have the range of...elks and...wild goats, and we show both flora and the fauna here. On the lake; we have swans, geese, ducks and, as the old folks say, "a power of birds." As they would say, "far as the eye could see, and farther." A *cloud* of birds. Flying. *(pause)* We have the *villages...*and *hamlets...*here and there the various small *farms.* The outposts, religious encampments...water mills. Much cattle. Horned cattle, and horses...these are marked by blue. For instance, we see in *this* district, the blue laid on thick. There were great herds here, and each individual household kept, on the average, three horses. *(Goes to the next map.)* And here twenty five years have passed. Already we see only one-third of the area is timbered. Goats are gone. We still see elk, occasionally, but the blue and green are vanishing. And so on. As we go down to the *third* rendition, *(Goes to the next map.)* where we have the district as it is today. We have no solid green, just the occasional patch. The elk, and the swans and geese have disappeared. The grouse are gone. The game birds. And we find no trace of the old settlements. In short, here is a perfect picture of a gradual and relentless decay. Which, in ten or twelve more years will be totally complete. And the land will be dead. You say, fine. You say deep cultural influences are at work, and the old life must naturally give way to the new. And I would agree with you. If in place of decimated forests we had *industry,* and *railroads, schools* under construction...*Mills...*and if the populace were happier, better employed, in better health. But what do we have here...? We have the same swamps and the same mosquitos. The same lack of roads, the same typhus, diptheria, rickets, diseases of poverty, the same eternal *fires*...So that what we *see* is this; a struggle for existence that is beyond human strength. Where we degenerate. In ignorance. And sloth. And so man, freezing, starving, diseased *man,* to preserve the last vestige of his life, to save his children, reaches out *reflexively* to stave his hunger, warm him, feed him, in his animal fear, and *destroys.* With no thought for tomorrow. So that nearly every thing has been destroyed. And nothing new brought into being...I see that this doesn't interest you.

YELENA ANDREYEVNA. But...I understand so little of it.

ASTROV. Ah. Apart from that though, it holds no interest for you.

YELENA ANDREYEVNA. I must tell you that my mind's on other things.

ASTROV. I see.

YELENA ANDREYEVNA. Forgive me.

ASTROV. Not at all...

YELENA ANDREYEVNA. And what *preoccupied* me was, in fact; I don't know how to begin.

ASTROV. ...please.

YELENA ANDREYEVNA. It was. *(pause)* An interrogation.

ASTROV. An interrogation?

YELENA ANDREYEVNA. Yes. A harmless one, if I may. Will you sit down? This concerns a certain *friend* of mine. A young friend. May we, do you think, as people of the world, may we speak frankly?

ASTROV. Of course.

YELENA ANDREYEVNA. And that the things we say we never spoke of? Do you understand?

ASTROV. I do.

YELENA ANDREYEVNA. The matter concerns my step-daughter, Sonya.

ASTROV. Yes.

YELENA ANDREYEVNA. How do you feel about her?

ASTROV. I respect her.

YELENA ANDREYEVNA. And your feelings for her as a woman.

ASTROV. My feelings of her...

YELENA ANDREYEVNA. Yes.

ASTROV. I have none.

YELENA ANDREYEVNA. Aha. Two more words and I'm done. Have you, perhaps, "remarked" her "attitude" towards you?

ASTROV. No. *(pause)*

YELENA ANDREYEVNA. Well, then, I'm done. You don't *love* Sonya, and *will* not. Now; she is *suffering*. And I ask your compassion, and that you stop coming here.

ASTROV. Uh huh...Uh huh...Well...it's late. I see that I've *stayed*...I really don't have the *time* to come here...If you...

YELENA ANDREYEVNA. Oh, Lord, what a sordid interview. Forgive me. It upsets me so, I feel as if I'd just worked two days in the fields. Well, we're finished. Thank God it's done and we never spoke of it at all. Fine. And now you must leave. *You* see that...Well, my goodness. I've turned quite red...

ASTROV. If even one *month* ago you have approached me...

YELENA ANDREYEVNA. ...No...

ASTROV. ...Yes. Then I might have considered it. And, if she's *suffering,* of course; if the girl's "suffering"... *(pause)* Aaahhh. *(pause)* I understand. *(pause)*

YELENA ANDREYEVNA. You understand what?

ASTROV. To belabor the obvious, when you know how one has to feel. Towards Sonya. Yet you call me here for an "interrogation..."

YELENA ANDREYEVNA. I don't understand.

ASTROV. *Oh* yes...*Oh* yes...and I walk into your trap.

Didn't I, now...? All *worry* over the poor girl's feelings. "What do you feel, as a man, dear doctor?" "Why have you been *coming* here the whole month, every day? Could we know your true feelings?" Alright! Alright!...I'll *tell* you, and *without* the charade. I confess it. I'm yours. I *surrender,* I'm *yours,* take me away.

YELENA ANDREYEVNA. Are you out of your mind?

ASTROV. Oh, *Lord,* you're timid! I've *confessed* it. Your sweet ruse has *forced* it out of me!

YELENA ANDREYEVNA. I'm going to tell you something. I am better than you think, I'm *nobler* than you think and I *swear* it to you.

ASTROV. Alright. I take my leave of you. This is the last of me. *(He glances around to insure that they are alone.)* Where shall we meet? Quickly. Say it. Quickly. While we have a moment. Where do we meet? And one kiss.

YELENA ANDREYEVNA. ...I swear before God...

ASTROV. Ah...Ah...Ah...Ah...Ahh...!!!!!! No need to swear. No need for words at all. How beautiful you are. Your face...

YELENA ANDREYEVNA. Oh, no. Please. *Please* go away.

ASTROV. You tell me where we're going to meet tomorrow. Tell me.

YELENA ANDREYEVNA. No.

ASTROV. It's *over.* It's *decided. Tell* me.

YELENA ANDREYEVNA. Have pity on me.

ASTROV. *I* surely *won't.*

YELENA ANDREYEVNA. Please leave me.

ASTROV. By the orchard. Two o'clock. Yes.

(VANYA Enters and looks at them as ASTROV embraces YELENA ANDREYEVNA.)

YELENA ANDREYEVNA. Let me go. Please. Let me go. *(She sees VANYA.)* Oh, God. *(pause)*

IVAN PETROVICH. Very well. *(pause)* Never mind it.

ASTROV. And *today*, my dear friend...the *weather*, wouldn't you say, the *weather*, which looked so cloudy, formerly... *(pause)* Is changed and the sun is out in what we must say's turned into a splendid afternoon. *(pause)* Winter *crops* are quite good, actually... *(pause)* Only mark against it is the *days* grow short, and what can *anyone* do about that?

YELENA ANDREYEVNA. *(to IVAN PETROVICH:)* I would *entreat* you, please, to exercise all of your *influence* to see that my husband and I *quit* this place at once. This afternoon. Do you hear?

IVAN PETROVICH. Yes.

YELENA ANDREYEVNA. Do you hear me? Today.

IVAN PETROVICH. Well, yes. You know, Helene, I saw the whole thing.

YELENA ANDREYEVNA. ...tell me you heard what I said.

IVAN PETROVICH. ...mmm...

YELENA ANDREYEVNA. We are leaving here today.

(Enter SEREBRYAKOV, SOFYA, TELEGIN and MARINA.)

TELEGIN. You know, your Excellency, I *myself* am feeling somewhat other-than-well. For the last two days; my head, my head *especially* does not feel well.

SEREBRYAKOV. Where are the others? I...where *are* they...? I hate this house, eh? Why should I live in a labyrinth? Twenty-six rooms, everybody *wandering*...

(RINGS.)

SEREBRYAKOV. Please ask the others in here.

YELENA ANDREYEVNA. ...I believe they're here.

SEREBRYAKOV. Ladies and gentlemen, be seated, please.

SOFYA. *(to YELENA ANDREYEVNA:)* What did he say?

YELENA ANDREYEVNA. ...Not now.

SOFYA. You're trembling. Are you trembling? That *is* it? *(pause)* Aha. Oh. *(pause)* I understand. *(pause)* He won't be staying around here anymore. *(pause)* That's it...yes? Tell it to me. Yes? *(YELENA ANDEYEVNA nods.)*

SEREBRYAKOV. *(to TELEGIN:)* You know, a man could reconcile himself to ill-health. But I cannot learn to live the country life. I can't stand it. I feel like I've spun off the earth and landed...Sonya! *(She doesn't hear him.)* Sonya! And, fine! *She* ignores me. Nurse, you come here, too. Please? *(To the nurse, who is just passing through and is motioned to sit. She does so.)* And now, if you please; ladies and gentlemen, if you could, if I may, like the *sunflower* turn your attentive heads...thank you...

IVAN PETROVICH. ...If it's the case that I'm not *needed* here...

SEREBRYAKOV. Oh, no, you're needed here. You have all.

IVAN PETROVICH. Then, if it please you, what do you require?

SEREBRYAKOV. "Please?" "Require?" Why, are you *angry?* Are you mad at me? If I am guilty, I beg your forgiveness.

IVAN PETROVICH. Fine. Fine. What do you want? What is it?

SEREBRYAKOV. And here is Maman! *(pause)* Ladies and gentlemen, now I will begin. "I have *summoned* you here, citizens, to *inform* you that the Inspector General has chosen to pay us a visit." *(pause)* Joking aside, then, in a *serious* vein, I have asked you here for your help and advice, knowing your graciousness, in full hope that I shall receive them. *(pause)* I am a *scholar.* I'm a man of books, and have long been a stranger to the intricacies, the *vagaries* of a business life. I could not live without the help and guidance of practical folk. And that is true. And so I come to you, Ivan Petrovich, Yelena, Ilya Iylich...Maman...an old man, not a well man who sees, from his age, *manet omnes una nox,* that time and tide happen to us all; and, at the *end* of his life, turns to *regulate* the questions of his property insofar as they touch and concern those around him; his family. *(pause)* My life is finished. But I possess a young *wife,* a daughter, still a *child... (pause)* And for us to continue living in the country is not possible. We are not made to live a country life. And *neither* can we live in town on income of the magnitude which this estate provides. Now, we could, for example, sell the *forest.* a measure which is both extreme, and non-renewable. Once sold, it yields no further income. So. Where could we seek to find a strategy which provides us with both a *definite* and, still, a *permanent* means of support? I have searched for and, I think, found that strategy. And, now, I have the honor of presenting it to you. In broad strokes; in general outline; our estate yields, on the average, a gain of, say, two percent. *(pause)* I propose to sell it. If we sell the estate and invest in interest-bearing bonds, we receive *four-to-five* percent. *Four-to-five.* And, I think that we should even have a *surplus* of sufficient funds to purchase a villa in Finland. *(pause)*

IVAN PETROVICH. Uh, excuse me. I'm sorry. Would you repeat what you said?

SEREBRYAKOV. I will, with the proceeds, invest in interest-bearing bonds, and, with such residue as there is, purchase a small home in Finland.

IVAN PETROVICH. Yes. No. Not the "Finland" part. You said the "proceeds." The proceeds of what?

SEREBRYAKOV. My sale of the estate.

IVAN PETROVICH. You're going to sell the estate.

SEREBRYAKOV. I propose to sell it. Yes.

IVAN PETROVICH. Ah. You see, that was the thing that caught my attention. You're going to sell the "estate?" And where do I go...? And *Sonya* here? Please? And my *mother,* if I may be so picayune...

SEREBRYAKOV. Certainly. All in good time. One can't do everything at once...

IVAN PETROVICH. No. One can *not.* You know, speaking of human ignorance. I always *supposed* that this "estate" which you're going to sell, belonged to Sonya...

SEREBRYAKOV. ...I...

IVAN PETROVICH. ...If I may, as my late *father* bought this estate as a dowry for my *sister,* so that it passed, in my *ignorance* to look upon the *law,* from my *sister* to *Sonya,* to whom it belongs.

SEREBRYAKOV. And who disputes it? *Certainly.*

IVAN PETROVICH. ...I...

SEREBRYAKOV. Of course. It belongs to Sonya. Without whose consent one could not think to sell it. And...*and* for whose benefit it shall be *sold.* *(pause)* For Sonya.

IVAN PETROVICH. *(simultaneously with "SONYA")* Am I out of my mind? Am I *raving...?* Why are we *listening* to...??

MARIYA VASILYEVNA. ...Jean...Jean...

IVAN PETROVICH. ...Why...?

MARIYA VASILYEVNA. Please. Don't, don't contradict Alexandr. *Please* believe me, he sees *far* better than we, what is *right,* what is...

IVAN PETROVICH. Someone give me a glass of water. *(drinks it)* Say whatever you wish to say. Say whatever you wish.

SEREBRYAKOV. Why do you *inflame* yourself? Do I say that my plan is *ideal?* It's a *"plan."* It's just a plan. And, if it's found *unsuitable,* I shall discard it. *(pause)*

TELEGIN. Your Excellency...?

SEREBRYAKOV. ...please...

TELEGIN. I myself, as I think you know, possess over and above my rev'rence for your *learning*...

SEREBRYAKOV. ...Yes...

TELEGIN. ...A feeling of kinship as well. Which brings me close to you. My brother, as I think you know, Grigory Ilyich, his *brother-in-law,* Fustian Trofich Lakidomov... held a degree...

IVAN PETROVICH. If you please, Waffles, not now.

TELEGIN. A degree, as I say, an M.A...

IVAN PETROVICH. ...We're talking business.

TELEGIN. Alright.

IVAN PETROVICH. Ask him.

SEREBRYAKOV. What am I to ask him?

IVAN PETROVICH. The estate was purchased from his uncle.

SEREBRYAKOV. *Was* it now...?

IVAN PETROVICH. Yes. It was, for the price, at that time. Yes. It was. Yes. For the price of ninety-five thousand roubles. Of which my father paid down seventy. Leaving a debt outstanding of 25. Now, are you following this? Because this estate could not have been bought had I not *renounced* my share, eh? Of my inheritance. In favor of my sister whom I dearly loved. And *additionally*. And *additionally* had I not toiled like an *ox,* as I have, working here ten years to discharge the remaining debt. Which I have done.

SEREBRYAKOV. ...I'm sorry that I brought it up...

IVAN PETROVICH. ...An cleared the estate. Which stands free-and-clear, thanks to *me!* Thanks to my efforts. And here you walk *in* here and propose throwing me out in the snow.

SEREBRYAKOV. I don't understand what you're trying to accomplish.

IVAN PETROVICH. I have managed this estate 25 years. I have slaved and sent you money like the Good Steward. *During* all that time not *once* have you thought to think of the man who worked for you. Not once. Twenty five years, you have *paid* me the magnificent sum of five hundred roubles a year. Five hundred roubles a year. And not *once* did it occur to you you might increase it.

SEREBRYAKOV. ...Ivan Petrovich...

IVAN PETROVICH. ...Twenty-five years...

SEREBRYAKOV. ...Ivan Petrovich. I am not a practical

man. You could have raised it any time you chose.

IVAN PETROVICH. I see. I should have stolen. and you despise me because I am not a thief. I *should* have stolen, and I wouldn't be a pauper now.

MARIYA VASILYEVNA. ...Jean...

TELEGIN. Vanya, my friend; *words,* words which are...I *beg* you...My dear friend. Why ruin good relations?

IVAN PETROVICH. *(simultaneous with "relations")* 25 years I've lived like a mouse in the wall. My mother and I. Our thoughts and our feelings turned toward you alone. We *talked* of you by day, of your works, of our *pride* in you. Uttered your name in awe. Our nights were spent reading your periodicals. You "publications" which now fill me with disgust.

TELEGIN. Vanya. Don't. Please. I can't...

SEREBRYAKOV. I don't understand what you think you want.

IVAN PETROVICH. You were a *magic being* and we knew your words by heart. My eyes have opened now. You write about Art. You understand *nothing* of art. You have no soul. You are a philistine. A fraud. A *swine,* feeding on the leavings of your betters...you...

SEREBRYAKOV. ...I beg you, make him stop. I'm leaving.

IVAN PETROVICH. ...You *bilked* us.

YELENA ANDREYEVNA. Ivan Petrovich. I insist you stop. Do you hear me...?

IVAN PETROVICH. No. No I *won't* stop. *(SEREBRYAKOV tries to leave the room. VANYA stops him.)* Wait. I'm not *done.* I'm not finished. You have ruined my life. I lost the best years of my life. For you. You assassin. You *thief.* You ruined my life.

TELEGIN. I cannot...I...I...I...I'm going. *(Exits.)*

SEREBRYAKOV. What is it that you want, and how can you *speak* to me like that? What *right* do you have? *Nothing.* You're *nothing.* You want the estate?' It's yours...? *Take* it. Take it. I've no need of it.

YELENA ANDREYEVNA. I can't stand this hell. Do you hear me? I can't bear it any longer. I'm leaving.

IVAN PETROVICH. My life is ruined. My life is a waste. And I have ruined it all. Talent, intelligence, courage. I could have been a Schopenhauer, I could have been the new Dostoyevsky, I could have designed a new *philosophy*...what am I saying? I'm losing my *mind* ...Mama. *Mama. Help me.* I'm in such pain...Mama!

MARINA. Do as Alexandr says.

SOFYA. Nanny...

IVAN PETROVICH. Mama! Mmmmmmmmmmwhat am I to do? *Tell* me. *Tell* me? *I* know. *Alright* then... *(to SEREB-RYAKOV:)* You think you'll *forget* me... *(Leaves the room, MARIYA VASILYEVNA follows him.)*

SEREBRYAKOV. My friends. Inform me what is going on. Take him away from me. Am I supposed to live under one roof with that? He lives right *here*... *(Points to VANYA'S door.)* Move him *away* from me. Now. To the *village*...to one of the *outbuildings.* Now, or *I* shall have to move, and I will. You hear me? But I will not live in this *house* with that man.

YELENA ANDREYEVNA. We're leaving today. Please. *(generally)* May we start the arrangements? Please?

SEREBRYAKOV. ...That *nothing* of a man. *(SOFYA falls to her knees.)*

SOFYA. Please. Papa. Please. Be merciful. Please. We are so unhappy. Uncle and I. Please. Be charitable. You remember when we were young. Uncle and I spent our nights translating your books for you. You remember? Copying out your texts...All those nights. All those nights we spent. Uncle Vanya and I. We worked without rest. We didn't spend a *kopek* on ourselves. *We sent it all to you.* We worked, Papa. We *earned* our bread. It's coming out wrong, no, but, Papa. I'm saying, it's *wrong,* but, hear what I'm saying, Papa, please, understand us. Be charitable...

YELENA ANDREYEVNA. *(simultaneous with "charitable")* Alexandr. Have it out. You have it all out wiht him now. I beg you. *(pause)* I beg you.

SEREBRYAKOV. Very well.

YELENA ANDREYEVNA. *Thank* you.

SEREBRYAKOV. ...I shall talk to him.

YELENA ANDREYEVNA. *Yes.*

SEREBRYAKOV. Did I accuse him?

YELENA ANDREYEVNA. No.

SEREBRYAKOV. What have I accused him of?

YELENA ANDREYEVNA. Nothing.

SEREBRYAKOV. I am not *angry* with him. But his actions...his actions towards me, we must say, charitably, they are *strange.* How...? *(pause)* I'll...Very well...to please you. I'll go speak to him.

YELENA ANDREYEVNA. Be gentle with him. Be calm. Try to calm him. *(Exits.)*

SOFYA. ...Nanny...

MARINA. Shhh. Shhh. Hush, hush, my child, the geese cackle, the geese cackle, then they stop. They cackle, then they stop.

SOFYA. ...Nanny...

MARINA. Shhhh. Shhhh. Stop shivering. Are you *cold?*
No? *Well,* then! There, there, dear orphan girl...God is a
merciful God. *(pause)* A little linden tea. Some rasp-
berries and tea and, then, it will pass. Sshhh. Shhh.
Shhhh. Little Orphan Girl. You geese! *Stop* it! Stop it,
now!

(A SHOT offstage.)

MARINA. Oh God!

(SEREBRYAKOV Enters.)

SEREBRYAKOV. Stop him, stop him, he's gone mad!

*(IVAN PETROVICH Enters with a revolver, YELENA
ANDREYEVNA tries to take it away from him.)*

YELENA ANDREYEVNA. Give it to me. *Give* it to me. Give
me the *gun,* I tell you...

IVAN PETROVICH. No! Helene! Let me go! Where is
he...? Ah! *(Sees SEREBRYAKOV, shoots.)* Bang! No? *Alright!*
Alright! Again, one more? *(Tries to fire, finds gun empty.)* No?
No? Oh, Damn...dámn...this... *(pause)* Damn... *(Bangs the
revolver on the floor, sits on a chair in exhaustion. YELENA
ANDREYEVNA leans against the wall, almost fainting.)*

YELENA ANDREYEVNA. Kill me. Take me away from here,
or dill me, but I can't stay here. *(pause)* I can't.

IVAN PETROVICH. ...Oh. What do I think I'm doing...?

SOFYA. ...Nanny...

(END OF ACT THREE)

ACT IV

SCENE: Ivan Petrovich's room. An autumn evening. Stillness.

AT RISE: TELEGIN and MARINA sit facing each other. Winding wool.

TELEGIN. If you want to finish it you'd better hurry.

MARINA. There's not much left.

TELEGIN. They'll be calling us soon.

MARINA. Umm hmmm

TELEGIN. ...To say goodbye. *(pause)* They've already called down for the horses.

MARINA. There's not much left.

TELEGIN. They're going to Kharkov. To live there.

MARINA. So much the better.

TELEGIN. They had a bad trauma here. Yelena Andreyevna says "I do not want to stay here." She keeps saying "we must go. We'll stay in Kharkov for awhile," she says, "to have a look around, and then send for our things." *They're* travelling light.

MARINA. ...mmm...

TELEGIN. It *seems*, Marina Timofeyevna, that they're not *predestined* to be living here. *(pause)* False predestination.

MARINA. ...so much the better.

TELEGIN. ...a scene worthy of an artist's pen.

MARINA. My old eyes cannot stand it. *(Pause, sighs.)* Well, we'll live again. As we used to. I know we will. In the old ways. With tea at seven and dinner at twelve and evening we sit down to supper. As we always did. As Christians. *(pause)* I haven't tasted simple human noodles in a long, long time, black with sin as I am...

TELEGIN. Yes. Quite a while since we've had noodles. *That's* true. *(pause) Quite* a long while. This morning, Marina Timofeyevna, this morning. I'm walking through the village, a *shopkeeper* shouts after me. "Hey, Freeloader!" Hey Deadbeat... *(pause)* And how did I feel then?

MARINA. Don't pay no mind to them, my darling, for we're all freeloaders in the sight of God. Living on nothing. Sonya, Ivan Petrovich...you, all of us. Sits about doing not one blessed thing, the while the whole world toils. Where's Sonya?

TELEGIN. Sonya, is in the garden with the doctor. Still looking for Ivan Petrovich.

MARINA. ...are they...?

TELEGIN. Afraid that he might lay hands on himself.

MARINA. And where's his pistol?

TELEGIN. Hid it in the root cellar.

MARINA. *Mercy...*

(IVAN PETROVICH and ASTROV Enter from the yard.)

IVAN PETROVICH. Leave me alone. *(To MARINA and TELEGIN.)* Will you leave me, please? Will you leave me...? If only for an hour? Oh. Please! Will you spare me this bodyguard...?

TELEGIN. Of course, Vanya.

MARINA. The Gander "Ga Ga Ga..!"

IVAN PETROVICH. Leave me.

ASTROV. For my part, with the greatest joy. Ought to have left a decent time ago. As I said, though, I *will* not do so, till you return what you took from me.

IVAN PETROVICH. I took nothing from you.

ASTROV. I'm speaking to you in all frankness; do not detain me. I should have left *long* ago.

IVAN PETROVICH. I took nothing from you. What are you saying...?

ASTROV. Eh? Alright. Eh? If you wish, I'll *sit* here for awhile and, then, if you *oblige* me, *subdue* you and *bind* you and *search* you. My word on it.

IVAN PETROVICH. As you wish. And the *worst* of it, the fool of the world, is to've shot *twice* and *twice missed* him. Which I cannot forgive myself. *Never.*

ASTROV. If the mood for shooting struck you, why not shoot *yourself...?*

IVAN PETROVICH. Myself. Mm. Hmm. *I'll* tell you an oddity: A man, myself, attempts murder, and do they arrest him? No. Why? *Obviously,* as I am regarded as insane. Ha. I am thought mad. But, a man who cloaks his heartlessness, his cruelty, and his, his *swinishness,* if you will, a man, hides behind a veil of false *achievement,* this wizard, this *genius*, this *exploiter, he* is not mad...A young woman who *marries* this old man, and when, in the sight of the world, betrays him. *I* saw what you did...

ASTROV. That's right. I did, and you can go to hell.

IVAN PETROVICH. ...And you. *You* are not mad. It is the *earth* which is mad to support you.

ASTROV. Quite poetic.

IVAN PETROVICH. Yes, well, I'm a madman, and I'm not responsible.

ASTROV. Mm.

IVAN PETROVICH. I can say what I wish.

ASTROV. *That's* a lovely trick.

IVAN PETROVICH. *Is* it...?

ASTROV. You're *not* mad, you know...

IVAN PETROVICH. What am I?

ASTROV. You're a fool. Time I thought, I used to think the foolish, the deranged, the irresponsible, are sick. They are not sick. They're normal. You are quite well.

IVAN PETROVICH. Oh, God, I am so ashamed. *(pause)* You cannot know the shame I feel. God. How can I stand it? How can I live with it? Tell me. What am I to do?

ASTROV. Nothing.

IVAN PETROVICH. Give me something to take. Oh *God.* I am *forty seven years of age.* If I live 'til *sixty* I will have to live *thirteen more years!* How can I live through that? What can I do? I've nothing to do with those years. You see? You see? If I could start *anew.* If I could live the rest of my life out in some different *way,* if that were possible. As people do, to *wake,* to waken each day and say, "this is a new day." If I could *lose* the past...how could I do that? Tell me. How could a man start anew? And begin a new life?

ASTROV. Oh, will you *shut up?* Will you go away! What are you *plaguing* me with? To start anew!? We can not "start anew." You or I. This or that, that we're living, you know, is our *life. (pause)*

IVAN PETROVICH. It is?

ASTROV. Quite. *(pause)*

IVAN PETROVICH. Give me something. *(Points to his heart.)* I have a pain. Here.

ASTROV. Oh *stop* it! *(pause)* Listen to me. People who live after us. In one hundred or in two hundred years, you know? Do you know what they'll feel? They will despise us for our stupid and insipid lives. And perhaps they will know how to be happy. We, however, but for you and I, there is but one hope. And that hope is this. That when we are dead, lying in our graves, visions may visit us, and that they are of peace. Oh, yes. My friend, we've said, in this district we find but two decent cultivated men. And we spoke of ourselves. But the last decade has undone us. Life has sucked us in. This foul, philistine life, and has corrupted us. What a shocking surprise; we've turned out like the rest! But we have changed the subject. Give me what you took.

IVAN PETROVICH. I took nothing.

ASTROV. You took a large bottle of morphia from my medicine case. If you are set on killing yourself, take your gun and go off in the woods. But give me back the drug, or people will say I gave it to you. It's enough I'll have to pronounce you dead and cut you open. Can you think I'll *enjoy* that...?

IVAN PETROVICH. Leave me alone.

(Enter SOFYA.)

ASTROV. Sofya Alexandrovna; your uncle has filched a vial of morphia from me and he won't give it back.

SOFYA. Is this true?

ASTROV. It *is* true. Please tell him it's rather *dowdy* of him, if nothing else, and that I must leave and must have it returned.

SOFYA. Give it back, Uncle. Why must you frighten us? Give it back. *(A pause.)* Uncle Vanya; am I more happy than you? *(A pause.)* Am I? Do I go about despairing? I *bear* my life, and *shall* till my life comes to its natural end. And so must you, Please. Give it back. Give it up to me. Sweet Uncle. Give it back. Please. Sweet one. Please. Be kind. You, who are so kind. Take pity on me. Give the bottle back. *(pause)* Uncle...

IVAN PETROVICH. Oh, *take* the thing. *Here. (Hands the bottle to her.)* I need *work.* I must *work,* do you understand me...?

SOFYA. Yes.

IVAN PETROVICH. I must turn my *hand* to something. *Now.* And I can't...

SOFYA. Yes. I understand. As soon as they've gone...We'll...

IVAN PETROVICH. Yes...

SOFYA. We'll sit down and...

IVAN PETROVICH. Yes. Yes...

SOFYA. We'll. We'll...

ASTROV. Thank you. Thank you all, and, now, I'm on my way.

(YELENA ANDREYEVNA Enters.)

YELENA ANDREYEVNA. Ivan Petrovich. Are you here? Please go to Alexandr. He has something he wishes to say.

SOFYA. Go, Uncle Vanya. Come, we'll go in together. You and Papa *have* to make it up. You know that. *(SOFYA and IVAN PETROVICH Exit.)*

YELENA ANDREYEVNA. I'm leaving. *(pause)* Goodbye.

ASTROV. Leaving. Already?

YELENA ANDREYEVNA. The horses are here.

ASTROV. Goodbye.

YELENA ANDREYEVNA. Today you promised me you'd move away from here.

ASTROV. Yes. I remember. I will. Presently. *(pause)* You're frightened.

YELENA ANDREYEVNA. Yes.

ASTROV. Then stay. *(pause)* Stay. Stay. And tomorrow at the orchard...

YELENA ANDREYEVNA. No, we're going. Which is the reason I can look at you. One thin, I should like you, when you think of me, to think well of me. If you can. *(pause)* I should like you to respect me.

ASTROV. I beg you to stay. I *beg* you to stay. Admit it, there's not one thing in the world for you to go to. Sooner or later you shall have to face the fact. In Kharkov, in Kursch, *somewhere.* Why not here? Right now. And just throw it up and begin again. Eh? *Right* now. Eh? In *such* a lovely autumn. We have *orchards*...we have run-down country *homes,* right out of Turgenyev...

YELENA ANDREYEVNA. Oh, you're funny. You're a funny man.

ASTROV. Am I...?

YELENA ANDREYEVNA. And I'm angry with you.

ASTROV. ...I'm sorry.

YELENA ANDREYEVNA. But I'll think of you with pleasure.

ASTROV. Why is that?

YELENA ANDREYEVNA. You're an original. We'll never

see each other again. I'll tell you — why hide it? — I was tempted by you. *(pause)* I was taken with you. *(pause)* So, good. Shake hands and part friends. Please. Don't think ill of me. *(They shake hands.)*

ASTROV. Yes. Goodbye, then. Mmmm...You know, I'll tell you something. This is strange. You see, I'm sure you *are* a good, warm-hearted person. But, yet what is there in your nature? Something. Here you come, you and your husband, and industrious people drop their work, neglect their duties, and waste whole *months* ministering to you, *talking* of you, buzzing around you, worrying for your husband's *gout*...your *wishes* for this and the other thing...And all become entangled in your idleness. How *is* that...? *I* was infected. One whole month, I haven't done a thing. People are falling ill, the peasants graze their cattle in my newly planted trees, all that I cared about's decaying. Your husband and you. Where you *light*... *(pause)* you seem to spread decay. I overstated myself. *(pause)* Yet...And, and, and, yet had you *stayed,* I feel something...something quite *terrible*...for me, for you, too, would have come to pass. *You* know it, *yes* you do. *You* know it, too. Ma! So. Finita la commedia! Go. And goodbye. *(YELENA ANDREYEVNA takes a pencil from ASTROV'S pocket.)*

YELENA ANDREYEVNA. I take this pencil as a memento.

ASTROV. Isn't that something? You come, we *meet,* suddenly you're gone and that's the way the world is, it seems. Do this, though, no one here, before Vanya comes back, with some bouquet for you. A kiss. One kiss. Yes? For goodbye. Yes? *(He kisses her.)* Alright then, *that's* done. That's done, and all's well.

YELENA ANDREYEVNA. I wish you all the best.

ASTROV. As I wish you.

YELENA ANDREYEVNA. Whatever...whatever.. *(pause)* Whatever...ah! For *once* in my life... *(She embraces him.)* I must go.

ASTROV. Well, go quickly. Your horses are ready. You had better go.

YELENA ANDREYEVNA. *(Hears noises, off.)* They're coming. I think...yes.

ASTROV. So be it. *(They embrace.)*

(Enter SEREBRYAKOV, IVAN PETROVICH, MARINA, TELEGIN and SOFYA.)

SEREBRYAKOV. Let bygones by bygones. I have lived through so much in these last four hours. I have *thought* so much. I feel I could compose a *treatise* for *posterity* on how one ought to live. I most *gladly* accept your apology, and I ask of you to accept mine as well. Farewell.

IVAN PETROVICH. You shall receive the same amount that you received before. Sent without fail and regularly. *Everything* shall be just as it was before. *(YELENA ANDREYEVNA embraces SONYA.)*

SEREBRYAKOV. Maman...

MARIYA VASILYEVNA. Alexandr, please sit for another photograph, and have it sent to me.

SEREBRYAKOV. I will.

MARIYA VASILYEVNA. How *precious* you are to me...

TELEGIN. Goodbye, your Ex'lency. Farewell. Don't forget us.

SEREBRYAKOV. Farewell. Farewell all... *(Shakes hands with*

ASTROV.) I thank you. For the pleasure of your company.
I possess nothing but the greatest respect for *you,* for your
way of *thinking,* for your *impulses* and your enthusiasm.
But I pray you, let an old man season his farewell with
one small observation. It's not enough to *think;* one must
work. Do you understand me...? Above all, the greatest
joy is to do some real *work* in the work world. Ladies and
gentlemen: All the best...I wish you all the *best*...and
goodbye. *(Exits, followed by MARIYA VASILYEVNA and
SONYA.)*

IVAN PETROVICH. Farewell. *(to YELENA ANDREYEV-
NA:)* Forgive me... *(Kisses her hand.)* We'll never meet
again.

YELENA ANDREYEVNA. Farewell, my dear, farewell.
(Kisses him on the head — Exits.)

ASTROV. Waffle.

TELEGIN. *Yes!*

ASTROV. While they're at it, tell them; bring my horses,
too.

TELEGIN. My friend, I will. *(Exits.)*

ASTROV. Not going to see them off?

IVAN PETROVICH. *(sighs)* Let them go where they're
going to. No, I...It's too hard. I'm going to turn my *hand*
to something. To some *work* eh?

*(IVAN rummages among papers in his desk. The sound of bells is
heard, receding.)*

ASTROV. ...and they're gone. Well, the *Professor* must be
thrilled. God *himself* couldn't lure that man back here.

(MARINA Enters.)

MARINA. They're gone.

(SOFYA Enters.)

SOFYA. They're gone. God grant them the best. Well. Uncle! *(pause)* Now. What shall we do?

IVAN PETROVICH. Work.

SOFYA. Yes.

IVAN PETROVICH. Absolutely. *(SOFYA sits at the desk.)*

SOFYA. What a long while since we've been together here. *(She lights the lamp on the desk.)* I think the ink is gone. *(pause)* Now they're gone I'm sad.

MARINA. ...They've gone. *(sits down)*

SOFYA. Alright. Uncle, first we'll catch up on our accounts. They're in a *wretched* state. A fellow wrote today, "This is the third time that I've asked you for my balance..." *(Starts passing out and sorting through papers.)* Alright, you do this one, I'll take the next, and so on...

IVAN PETROVICH. *(Reads paper, starts to write.)* "For the account of..." *(They write in silence for awhile.)*

MARINA. Well, I'm ready to go up to bed.

ASTROV. *(pause)* In the stillness, pens are scratching. The crickets chirp. Warm. Close. *(sighs)* No, I don't feel like leaving.

(A sound of BELLS is heard.)

ASTROV. Ah, my horses. Well. It seems that all it lacks is my "goodbye." I'm off, then.

MARINA. Stay awhile.

ASTROV. I can't.

IVAN PETROVICH. *(writing)* "...With the addition of the previous balance of eighty-seven roubles,...balance still remaining..."

(WORKMAN Enters.)

WORKMAN. Mikhail Lvovich, your horses are here.

ASTROV. Thank you. I heard them. *(Hands him portfolio and medicine case.)* Exercise extreme care with these, please, and with the portfolio.

WORKMAN. Yes. *(Exits.)*

ASTROV. Well...

SOFYA. When shall we see you again?

ASTROV. Not before summer I'd think. Hardly this winter. Of course, if you should *need* me...I thank you for your *kindness*...for your *hospitality.* Thank you for everything. *(He kisses the nurse on the head.)* And, old one, farewell.

MARINA. You haven't had your tea.

ASTROV. I don't want any.

MARINA. A vodka?

ASTROV. *(pause)* Perhaps a small one. *(MARINA goes out.)* I've got my *trace* horse limping. Don't know why. Noticed it yesterday when he was coming up.

IVAN PETROVICH. He needs reshoeing.

ASTROV. I'll stop by the farrier at Rozhdesrvennoe.

IVAN PETROVICH. *I* would...

ASTROV. No help for it. I would think down in *Africa* the heat must be *intense.*

IVAN PETROVICH. I think so.

(MARINA Enters with a glass of vodka and a small piece of bread on a tray.)

MARINA. *Here* you are...To your health, little father. Eat some bread with it.

ASTROV. No, no, I'm fine. Thank you, nurse. Don't see me off. Goodbye, all, the best to you. Goodbye. *(He goes out, SONYA goes after him with a candle to see him off.)*

IVAN PETROVICH. *(writes)* "The second *February.* Twenty pounds vegetable oil...The *sixteeth, fifteen* pounds... *(pause)* Buckwheat..."

(The sound of BELLS is heard.)

MARINA. He's gone.

(SOFYA reenters.)

SOFYA. He's gone.

IVAN PETROVICH. "...for a sub-total of...fifteen, twenty...twenty-five..." *(SONYA sits down and begins to write.)*

MARINA. *(yawns)* Mercy...

(TELEGIN Enters quietly, stands by the door, tunes his guitar. IVAN PETROVICH passes his hand over SONYA'S hair.)

IVAN PETROVICH. My child. How hard it is for me. If you knew how hard it is for me. You can't know.

—— SOFYA. But what can we do? All we can do is live. We'll live through a long row of days. And through the endless evenings. And we'll bear up. Under the trials fate has sent to us. We will constantly toil for others. Now, and the rest of our days. And when we come to die, we'll die submissively. *Beyond* the grave we will testify that we have suffered; that we've wept, and have known bitterness. And God will pity us. You and I. *(pause)* Dear Uncle, God will take pity on us. And *we,* Uncle, shall live a life of radiant beauty and grace. And look back on this life of our happiness with tenderness. And smile. And in that new life we shall rest. Uncle. I know it. I have faith. I have a passionate faith. We shall rest. *(pause)* We shall rest to the songs of the angels. In a firmament arrayed in jewels. And look down, and we will see evil, all the evil in the world, and all our sufferings, bathed in a perfect mercy, and our life grown sweet as a caress. I have faith. Oh...Poor Uncle Vanya. You're crying. I know. I know. You have had no joy in your life. But wait. And only wait, Uncle Vanya, we shall rest. *(She embraces him.)* We shall rest. *(The WORKMAN taps. TELEGIN plays softly on the guitar, MARIYA VASILYEVNA writes on her pamphlet. MARINA knits.)*

—— SOFYA. We shall rest.

(THE END)

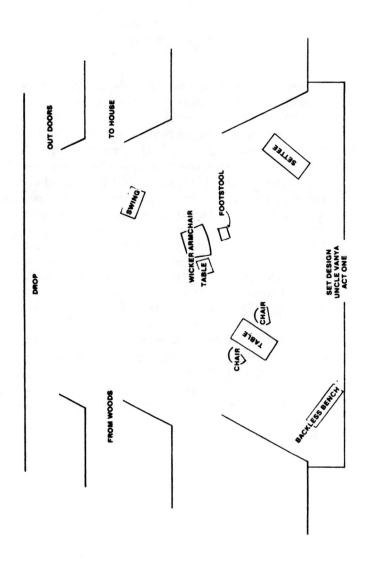

OUT DOORS

TO HOUSE

SWING

SETTEE

FOOTSTOOL

DROP

WICKER ARMCHAIR

TABLE

SET DESIGN
UNCLE VANYA
ACT ONE

CHAIR

TABLE

CHAIR

FROM WOODS

BACKLESS BENCH

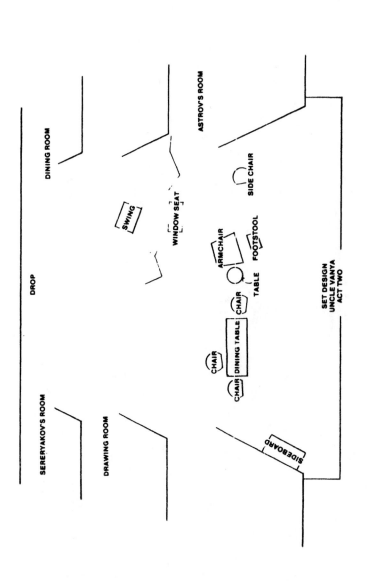

SERERYAKOV'S ROOM

DRAWING ROOM

DROP

DINING ROOM

ASTROV'S ROOM

SWING

WINDOW SEAT

SIDE CHAIR

ARMCHAIR

FOOTSTOOL

TABLE

CHAIR

DINING TABLE

CHAIR

CHAIR

SIDEBOARD

SET DESIGN
UNCLE VANYA
ACT TWO

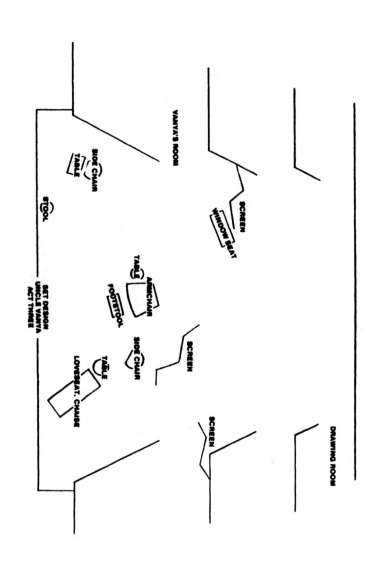

SET DESIGN
UNCLE VANYA
ACT THREE

VANYA'S ROOM

DRAWING ROOM

SIDE CHAIR
TABLE
STOOL
SCREEN
WINDOW SEAT
ARMCHAIR
TABLE
FOOTSTOOL
SIDE CHAIR
TABLE
LOVESEAT, CHAISE
SCREEN
SCREEN

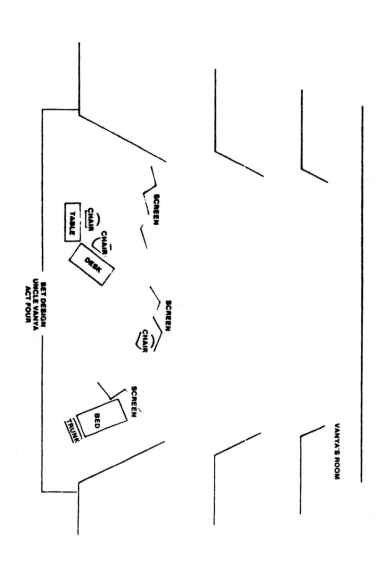

SET DESIGN
UNCLE VANYA
ACT FOUR

SCREEN

CHAIR
TABLE
CHAIR
DESK

SCREEN
CHAIR

SCREEN
BED
TRUNK

VANYA'S ROOM

Works by
David Mamet...

American Buffalo
Bobby Gould In Hell
The Cherry Orchard (Adapted by)
Dark Pony
Death Defying Acts
The Disappearance of the Jews
Dramatic Sketches and Monologues
The Duck Variations
Edmond
The Frog Prince
Glengarry Glen Ross
Goldberg Street
Keep Your Pantheon
Lakeboat
A Life in the Theatre
The Luftmensch
Mr. Happiness
November
The Old Neighborhood
One Way Street
The Poet and the Rent
Race
Reunion
The Sanctity of Marriage
School
Sexual Perversity in Chicago
The Shawl
Speed-the-Plow
Squirrels
The Three Sisters (Adapted by)
Uncle Vanya (Adapted by)
The Water Engine
The Woods

Please visit our website **samuelfrench.com** for complete
descriptions and licensing information.

OTHER TITLES AVAILABLE FROM SAMUEL FRENCH

THE POET AND THE RENT

David Mamet

Drama / 8m, 3f, extras (doubling possible) / Simple set

David, a young poet behind in his rent and about to be evicted, improvises poems for money in the park. He is scorned by the public and he falls in love with a young woman who will have nothing to do with him. He becomes a nightwatchman and is robbed by thieves who talk him into joining them. Apprehended by the police and jailed, he is visited by a man who heard his poems – an ad executive who offers David a job writing ad copy for Wacko, noxious gook for cars. Faced with his first existential choice, he decides to languish in jail rather than promote Wacko. The young woman pays his bail and rent. She still finds him socially undesirable, but feels all good citizens should support the arts. A better man, David returns to his pen and paper.

OTHER TITLES AVAILABLE FROM SAMUEL FRENCH

SPEED-THE-PLOW

David Mamet

Dramatic Comedy / 2m, 1f / 2 interiors, simply suggested

Revived on Broadway in 2008, the original production starred Joe Mantegna, Ron Silver and Madonna in this hilarious satire of Hollywood, a culture as corrupt as the society it claims to reflect. Charlie Fox has a terrific vehicle for a currently hot client. Bringing the script to his friend Bobby Gould, the newly appointed Head of Production at a major studio, both see the work as their ticket to the Big Time. The star wants to do it; as they prepare their pitch to the studio boss, Bobby wagers Charlie that he can seduce the temp/secretary, Karen. As a ruse, he gives her a novel by "some Eastern sissy" writer that needs a courtesy read before being dismissed out of hand. Karen slyly determines the novel, not the movie-star script, should be the company's next film. She sleeps with Bobby who is so smitten with Karen and her ideals that he pleads with Charlie to drop the star project and and pitch the "Eastern sissy" writer's book.

"Hilarious and chilling ."
– *The New York Times*

"Mamet's clearest, wittiest play."
– *The New York Daily News*

"I laughed and laughed. The play is crammed with wonderful, dazzling, brilliant lines."
– *The New York Post*